FDR'S
ALPHABET SOUP

New Deal America, 1932–1939

FDR'S ALPHABET SOUP

NEW DEAL AMERICA, 1932–1939

NRA   FERA
FDIC   AAA
AAA CCC   TVA
PWA
FERA
NRA

TONYA BOLDEN

ALFRED A. KNOPF   New York

For
Benjamin Nathaniel Aronson
Phillip Joseph Dismukes
Lucinda Dean Gunton
&
Greta Crail Mohr

Be
Lights
to the
World.

THIS IS A BORZOI BOOK PUBLISHED BY ALFRED A. KNOPF

Text copyright © 2010 by Tonya Bolden

All rights reserved. Published in the United States by Alfred A. Knopf, an imprint
of Random House Children's Books, a division of Random House, Inc., New York.

Illustration credits can be found on page 128.

Knopf, Borzoi Books, and the colophon
are registered trademarks of Random House, Inc.

Visit us on the Web! www.randomhouse.com/teens

Educators and librarians, for a variety of teaching tools,
visit us at www.randomhouse.com/teachers

Library of Congress Cataloging-in-Publication Data is available upon request.
ISBN 978-0-375-85214-5 (trade) — ISBN 978-0-375-95214-2 (lib. bdg.)

The text of this book is set in 11-point New Aster.

MANUFACTURED IN CHINA
January 2010
10 9 8 7 6 5 4 3 2 1

First Edition

In a game of cards, a new deal means the gathering up of every player's cards and the dealing out of new hands. A player's new cards may be better than those he has had, or they may be worse. They are certain to be different.

—Gertrude Van Duyn Southworth and John Van Duyn Southworth,
The New Deal: An Impartial History of the Roosevelt Administration (1935).

CONTENTS

February 1932: A breadline in NYC.

BROKE AND HUNGRY

Forty-five-year-old Albert Sacks preferred the Big House to freedom.

Convicted of grand larceny, Sacks had entered a New York State prison in 1928 and left in October 1931 on parole. Several months later, he was at that same prison's gates, begging to be let back in.

"Describing himself as 'broke and hungry,' he told the warden he had hitch hiked all the way from Cleveland." So said the AP (Associated Press). This news service also reported that the warden obliged. Sad Sacks became "a number again in the gray-clad legions of the prison."

Dateline: Auburn, New York, July 2, 1932. This was almost three years after the October 1929 stock market crash—year three of the Great Depression.

Millions of people were broke. Millions were hungry.

Like Albert Sacks, millions were both.

Some Hard-Times U.S. Stats (1929–1932)

- **Stocks lost** more than 75% of their value, wiping out some $45 billion in wealth.
- About 20% of the roughly 25,000 **banks failed** because of heavy losses in the stock market, real estate, and other investments; customer defaults on loans (including mortgages); and/or waves of withdrawals.
- **Depositors lost** more than $1 billion—some their life's savings—in bank failures.
- Roughly 300,000 other **businesses shuttered**—from butcher shops to steel mills—in large part because cash-poor and just plain scared consumers cut back on spending.

- **Unemployment among nonfarm workers tripled,** from about 4 million to about 12 million—nearly 25% of that workforce. First fired: young people, old people, people of color, and married women whose husbands had jobs.
- Some 600,000 **homes went into foreclosure.**
- **Net farm income fell** from over $6 billion a year to about $2 billion.
- **National income dropped** by more than 50% (from about $88 billion to about $42 billion).
- **Suicides rose** by more than 25% (from 13.9 per 100,000 to 17.4 per 100,000).

The day of that AP item on "broke and hungry" Albert Sacks was also the day of a political first: a presidential hopeful accepted his party's nomination in the flesh. He was New York's two-term Democratic governor, FDR.

Born rich and into the ruling class, FDR had never walked the hunger road, but he knew pain. Back in the summer of 1921, at age thirty-nine, this effervescent, ever-active man—who loved sailing, golfing, and horseback riding—was literally knocked off his feet.

Polio.

With his legs rendered useless, FDR got around in a wheelchair—mostly, not exclusively. He trained himself to grin and bear a way to walk short distances: wearing heavy steel leg braces and relying on crutches, a cane, or the strong arm of another.

1923: Warm Springs, Georgia. FDR began visiting this resort after he heard that its waters did wonders for another man with polio. FDR was up for trying everything—*anything*—to walk again. He later purchased the resort and made it a center for people with polio.

July 1889: Franklin Delano Roosevelt, age seven, living in Hyde Park, New York, on his parents' huge estate with so many wonders for this young nature lover to enjoy.

May 1905: Newlyweds in Newburgh, New York. FDR with his wife and distant cousin, ER (Eleanor Roosevelt). She was also born rich—and also knew grief. By age eleven, ER had lost both parents: her mother to diphtheria, her father to the ravages of alcohol and morphine addiction.

June 1919: Family portrait in D.C. *Standing, left to right:* FDR and ER's oldest surviving children, Anna, James, and Elliott. *On Daddy's knee:* Franklin Jr. *Opposite him:* John, on the lap of FDR's mother, Sara. (FDR's father, James, a financier-entrepreneur, had died in 1900.) When this photo was taken, FDR was assistant secretary of the navy. Before that, he was a New York state senator (1910–1913).

It was while FDR was its governor that the Empire State became the first in the nation to have a major helping-hand agency for people out of work: TERA (Temporary Emergency Relief Administration).

"The duty of the State toward the citizen is the duty of the servant to its master," FDR had told his legislature. He believed that governments ought to care for citizens in crisis—"not as a matter of charity but as a matter of *social duty.*"

In his bid for his party's nomination for the presidency, FDR pitched himself as the champion of what he called in one speech "the forgotten man at the bottom of the economic pyramid." Such a soul deserved a more gumptious government—a government gutsy enough to pull out all the stops. "The country needs and, unless I mistake its temper, the country demands bold, persistent experimentation," he asserted in another address. "It is common sense to take a method and try it: If it fails, admit it frankly and try another. But above all, try something."

November 1920: Loving a parade in Dayton, Ohio. FDR, VP pick (right), strides beside Democratic presidential candidate James Middleton Cox, governor of the Buckeye State. Cox and Roosevelt lost to the GOP's Harding-Coolidge ticket.

From the 1928 presidential race, in which Secretary of Commerce Herbert Clark Hoover trounced the Dems' Al Smith, at the time governor of New York and one of FDR and ER's political mentors.

During the GOP's national convention at Chicago Stadium in mid-June 1932, Republicans decided to try Herbert Hoover again.

Orphaned at age eight, Herbert Hoover worked his way up from poverty to become a mining engineer, then a millionaire through shrewd business moves. He was a Great American Success Story.

And the Great Engineer. People called Hoover that because of the relief effort he led in Europe following World War I (1914–1918). Later, for the rescue-and-recovery work he engineered after the catastrophic Mississippi River flood (1927), he was hailed as the Great Humanitarian.

Most Americans had high hopes for Hoover's presidency when he took the oath of office in March 1929—seven months before the crash. Praise plummeted as the Depression deepened. People now dumped on him as the Great Do-Nothing.

But Hoover had not done *nothing*. For one, he asked captains of industry to refrain from cutting jobs and wages (and was largely ignored). He urged strong banks to create a pool of

$500 million from which struggling ones could borrow, but the big banks chipped in only $10 million.

After that flop, Hoover signed off on a bill that created a new government agency, the RFC (Reconstruction Finance Corporation). Its mission: to lend money to businesses on the brink of collapse, most especially financial institutions. The RFC was funded with $500 million of taxpayers' dollars (and could borrow up to $1.5 billion from Treasury or from people or firms with deep pockets). The idea behind the RFC was that bailouts for businesses would trickle down to workaday folks.

As for them, Hoover felt it folly for the federal government to bail out *people* on the brink. That's what charities and family and friends were for. Hoover was a staunch believer in a small federal government, clinging to the idea that "rugged individualism" was the essence of the American way.

The president's name became a byword for hard times: empty pants pockets turned out were called Hoover flags; shantytowns of homeless people, Hoovervilles; and the hard times themselves—the Hoover Depression.

> **" Our president is still trying to give money to the bankers, but none to the people. If I had my way, it would go to the people, who need it badly. "**
>
> —January 1932: Father James Renshaw Cox of Pittsburgh, shortly before he led a multitude in a march on Washington for jobs.

October 1931: A Hooverville in Seattle.

What Caused the Great Depression?

It wasn't the stock market crash alone. On that, scholars agree. As debate rages about what caused the move from a recession (a thunderstorm) to a depression (a hurricane), some see it as a perfect storm. The elements include:

- **Stock market speculation:** In this unregulated sector, many stocks were wildly overvalued and hyped. People could buy stocks on margin—some putting as little as 10% down—and end up in huge debt if a stock was a dud.

- **Concentration of wealth:** Just 1% of the population had about 40% of the wealth. Economic good times depended on big spending and investment by a few.

- **The Smoot-Hawley Tariff Act (1930):** Congress raised taxes on imports, hoping to encourage more Americans to buy domestically made goods. Other nations retaliated with tariffs of their own. This made some U.S. goods too expensive for citizens elsewhere, so American farmers and manufacturers did less export business. (And U.S. agriculture was already in the dumps.)

- **A tightfisted Fed:** The Federal Reserve Bank—America's central bank and the lender of last resort—failed to offer cash-strapped banks low-interest emergency loans to stay afloat.

- **Overcapacity:** During the 1920s, many companies bulked up their operations (from physical plant and workforce to inventory), banking on perpetual prosperity and constant consumption. Similarly, many farmers expanded their acreage and bought tractors and other equipment, often on credit.

- **Consumer debt:** To keep demand apace with supply, want creation had increased. Ad agencies aced the art of convincing people of modest incomes that luxuries and conveniences were *necessities*. No money tree was needed because of the buy-now-pay-later scheme, the installment plan. It allowed people to do what future generations would do with credit cards: buy what they wanted—appliances, furniture, phonographs, radios, and more—when they wanted it, and make small payments over time, with interest accruing.

- **World debt from World War I:** America was the big creditor nation during the war, lending about $7 billion to its allies. After the war, America lent its allies another $3 billion for aid and reconstruction of their war-torn cities. As the world economy slowed down and the Depression became global, nobody—not Britain, France, or anyone else—could pay back Uncle Sam. And there was no way that Germany, the war's biggest loser, could pay off the $33 billion in reparations it owed various nations anytime soon.

"The Forgotten Man"

In the 1880s, philosopher William Graham Sumner coined the term "the Forgotten Man" for nose-to-the-grindstone middle-class folks who rock no boats, but who are often ignored and even shafted. When FDR applied the term to the down-and-out, conservatives charged him with inciting class warfare.

Two weeks after the Republicans picked Hoover—same city, same stadium—the Democrats picked FDR. He was at the governor's mansion in Albany when that late-night telephone call came from Chicago.

By tradition (a holdover from the horse-and-buggy days), major-party nominees didn't attend conventions and didn't deliver their acceptance speeches until weeks later, after official written notification. (Hoover would accept in mid-August.)

To heck with tradition, thought FDR. His message to conventioneers boiled down to *Please, sit tight!*

The next morning, July 2, he was aboard a small plane, a Ford Tri-Motor. About nine hours later, on the arm of son James, FDR made his leg-braced way to the podium.

The crowd was doubly wowed. Few civilians had ever flown.

From the *New York Daily Mirror* on the Fourth of July 1932.

"The appearance before a National Convention of its nominee for President, to be formally notified of his selection, is unprecedented and unusual, but these are unprecedented and unusual times," said FDR at the start of his speech. At the end, he made a vow to the thirty thousand conventioneers and to the roughly 120 million others around the nation, legions of whom were listening via radio.

With voice all vigor, FDR declared: "I pledge you, I pledge myself, to a new deal for the American people."

A MESSAGE OF HOPE

July 28, 1932: Soldiers forcing a Bonus Army contingent from an encampment near Pennsylvania Avenue in D.C. In charge: U.S. Army Chief of Staff Major General Douglas MacArthur, future president Dwight David "Ike" Eisenhower (then "Mac's" aide and a major), and Major George S. Patton Jr. ("Old Blood and Guts" in a few years' time).

2

KICK OUT DEPRESSION

FDR's new deal would need to be a B-I-G deal to combat quickening chaos and talk of revolution.

Some twenty thousand broke and hungry World War I vets—the "Bonus Army"—descended upon D.C. during the spring and summer of 1932. Colorado and Connecticut, Oregon and Oklahoma, Texas and Tennessee—they came from all over the place, packed into wing-and-a-prayer jalopies and teetering trucks, by freight train and on two feet. Their urgent plea to the government: early release of pension pay (a "bonus" not due until 1945 or death).

The Bonus Army didn't get what it came for. Its plight became more pitiable when a police action to boot some vets from downtown D.C. escalated into a military action, with troops poking protesters with bayonets, terrorizing them with tear gas, and torching their makeshift homes on the Anacostia Flats and elsewhere.

> **Mr. Licht at the Welfare said he couldn't help us, mister. Well, we're helping ourselves. You expect us to starve while there's food on the shelves?**
>
> —Circa 1931: A female member of a raid on an A&P in Van Dyke, Michigan.

Shortly after the Bonus Army was routed, Iowa farmers kicked up a ruckus—the Corn Belt Rebellion.

These farmers wanted higher prices for their corn, hogs, and other commodities. They were fed up with getting a pittance—sometimes less than their cost of production.

The Iowa farmers were up against the law of supply and demand: when supply exceeds demand, prices fall. (Farmers in other states had a supply problem: they were dealing with drought and dust-storm devastations and had little or nothing to sell, even at the prevailing low prices.)

"Stay at Home—Buy Nothing—Sell Nothing." This was the banner cry of those striking Iowa farmers. To thwart transport of farm produce, some militants blockaded highways, and clashes with cops broke out in spots. (Farmers in Nebraska and other area states also went on the warpath.)

Fired-up farmers were not new. By 1932, more than a few had used violence and the threat of violence to force sheriffs and judges to halt auctions of foreclosed farms—just as crowds of city dwellers did against landlords and lawmen trying to evict families whose rents were past due.

There had been food riots, too. Some mobs menaced merchants into handing out provisions. Others flat out looted.

The streets of state capitals as different as Springfield, Illinois, and FDR's Albany, New York, had also seen hunger marches. The outfit leading many of these protests was the NCUC (National Committee of Unemployed Councils USA). Its first national march came on December 7, 1931. During that march on Washington, NCUC petitioned Congress for unemployment insurance for *all* workers, no matter what their race, gender, or age.

This unemployment insurance was to be funded by (a) taxes on big business and on people making more than $5,000 a year (roughly $200,000 today) and (b) money spent on "war preparations" (the defense budget).

Another demand: "social insurance" for people who couldn't work because of "sickness, old age, maternity, etc." Added to this, NCUC lobbied the government to get moving on major emergency measures, such as a cash grant of $150 to every unemployed worker (plus $50 for each of that person's dependents). This, to tide folks over through the winter.

Also on the list: a moratorium on evictions; vets' bonuses; and urban renewal—the "immediate undertaking of extensive public works, particularly new houses, schools, hospitals, etc., in the working class neighborhoods."

The right to unionize: this was among the demands of marchers whom NCUC's Detroit unit led three months later, on a freezing March day.

Destination: the Ford Motor Company's huge complex in nearby Dearborn, Michigan, on the banks of the River Rouge.

Result: a bloodstained day.

With Ford's private cops as backup, the police stuck to their guns—literally—in busting up the protest. At day's end, several people were dead and dozens wounded.

NCUC was the work of American "Reds," members of the CPUSA (Communist Party USA), inspired by the outcome of the Russian Revolution (1917–1918): the Soviet Union, a communist federation of states.

Most American communists had gone underground after the first Red Scare (1919), with its jailings, deportations, and

This NCUC pamphlet was devoted to the 1931 National Hunger March.

> **" To bring on the revolution it may be necessary to work inside the Communist Party. "**
>
> —1932: Novelist F. Scott Fitzgerald.

ABCs of Some -Isms

- **Capitalism:** Individuals own the means of production, like auto plants and farms. The free market—that is, the law of supply and demand—determines wages and prices for goods and services.

- **Communism:** The people, collectively, own the means of production. Individuals contribute to society what they can and receive from society what they need.

- **Socialism:** The people, collectively, own the major means of production. What individuals receive from society is based on what they contribute. (The industrious can make more money than the lazy.)

- **Fascism:** The State is the master; the citizen, the servant.

Selling stamps like this was one way the ILD raised funds.

other acts of Uncle Sam's and citizens' wrath against radicals of all stripes, from tough talkers against capitalism to bomb throwers. During all that drama, many on the sidelines decided to steer clear of anything to do with leftist views.

Hard times soon changed that. More people questioned capitalism—and heaped plenty of blame for the Depression on the Three Bs: businessmen, brokers, bankers.

The Three Bs were painted with a broad brush as greedy fiends, because many business owners (and most were men) had denied workers raises when company profits were soaring during the Roaring Twenties.

Many brokers had pulled dishonest schemes and peddled lousy stocks. Few workaday people owned stocks, but when the bubble burst, masses lost their J-O-Bs as firms and families sucking up stock market losses tightened their belts.

As for the "banksters," a host of them had gambled away depositors' money on stocks. Added to that, too many banks had lax lending policies—and many people who borrowed money speculated on real estate and in the stock market.

So now, like other leftist groups, the CPUSA was attracting people up and down the socioeconomic ladder and across racial and ethnic lines. (Communists got a lot of sympathy after the River Rouge riot.)

More blacks gave the CPUSA a listen after its legal wing, the ILD (International Labor Defense), stood up for the "Scottsboro Boys": nine blacks (the oldest nineteen, the youngest thirteen) arrested near Scottsboro, Alabama, then stuck in prison—with eight facing the electric chair—because two white girls lied about being raped on a freight train.

Before, during, and after the railroading of the Scottsboro Boys, true crime was climbing. There were desperate have-nots robbing haves. There were scrapes *between* have-nots over scraps of food or choice spots by fires in hobo jungles and Hoovervilles.

Gangsters like Bonnie and Clyde, and Ma Barker's "boys," were still plotting and pulling off heists. Syndicates like Detroit's Purple Gang and the crew Lucky Luciano ruled in New York were having a heyday with gambling joints, prostitution rings, loan-sharking, and more. Thanks to Prohibition, mobsters did big business in bootleg booze, from smuggling to running speakeasies.

Up went the number of cops and politicians on the take. Up went the drive-by machine-gunnings and other acts of mayhem among gangs and between crooks and crime fighters.

By 1932, support for Prohibition was way down among the law-abiding. On top of kindling crime, Prohibition robbed the government of revenue it would have raked in from taxes on alcoholic beverages.

When FDR promised the nation a new deal, he also said that Prohibition was "doomed."

> **If I vote at all it will be for the Communists, in order to express as emphatically as possible the belief that our present crisis calls for a complete and drastic reorientation.**
>
> —1932: Cultural critic (among other things) Lewis Mumford.

August 1932: Peekskill, New York. FDR on the campaign trail with an ex-rival for the nomination, now his running mate: Speaker of the House John Nance Garner, a Texan known as Cactus Jack.

James Maurer was a former Pennsylvania legislator and president of the Pennsylvania Federation of Labor.

In July, Hoover signed off on a bill allowing the RFC to finance public works (up to $1.5 billion) and to lend states money for relief programs (up to $300 million). In his last major campaign speech, on October 31, at MSG, Hoover warned against "so-called new deals which would destroy the very foundations of the American system of life."

gets deeper and deeper in business for the sake of saving business." A vote for the Democratic Party was just a vote "for the same capitalistic system under slightly different trimming." Capitalism, said Thomas, was nothing but "glorified racketeering."

Thomas was no political rookie. Since 1924, he had run for several offices, including the presidency. Tireless Thomas had also co-founded the ACLU (American Civil Liberties Union) and, before that, the human rights organization that would launch the first Freedom Rides in the 1940s: the U.S. branch of FOR (Fellowship of Reconciliation).

Neither FDR nor Hoover was worried about Norman Thomas or any other third-party candidate. The Democratic and Republican parties had ruled politics since the mid-nineteenth century. Still, there were always third parties in the running, usually just seeking to raise the profile of unpopular (and often ridiculed) issues. Example: socialists were way ahead of most major-party politicians on women's suffrage (granted in 1920).

The Republican Party's nickname has stood for the "Gallant Old Party" and the "Grand Old Party." The major parties' symbols became a hit because of a captivating 1874 cartoon by the legendary Thomas Nast. In it, he depicted the Democratic Party as a deceitful donkey and the Republican Party as a scared elephant. Each party rejected the characterization but embraced the symbol.

FDR spent most of Election Day eve pressing the flesh in up-state New York, often talking to folks from atop the backseat of his car—flashing his spirit-lifting smile. Such a marvelous match with his theme song: "Happy Days Are Here Again."

In New York and across the nation, voters put their faith in FDR big-time. On November 8, he was president-elect.

Folks were on tiptoe for that new deal he had pledged.

WORK-IS-WHAT-I-WANT-AND-NOT-CHARITY-WHO-WILL-HELP-ME-GET-A-JOB-7 YEARS-IN-DETROIT. NO-MONEY-SENT-AWAY-FURNISH-BEST-OF-REFERENCES. PHONE RANDOLPH 8381 Room

ELECTION RETURNS

Candidate	Electoral Votes	Popular Votes
Foster	0	102,785
Thomas	0	881,951
Hoover	59	15,758,901
FDR	472	22,809,638

Only six of the country's forty-eight states went for Hoover: Connecticut, Delaware, Maine, New Hampshire, Pennsylvania, and Vermont.

> **Many essential public services have been reduced beyond the minimum point absolutely essential to the health and safety of the city. . . . The salaries of city employees have been twice reduced . . . and hundreds of faithful employees . . . have been furloughed. . . . For the coming year, Detroit can see no possibility of preventing wide-spread hunger and slow starvation.**

—1932: A Detroit city official.

A 1932 mechanical pin.

FIFTEEN CENTS IN CANADA 20.
January 2, 1933

TIME

The Weekly Newsmagazine

Photographed in Natural Color by O. J. Jordan

Volume XXI

MAN OF THE YEAR
He climbed a hill of beans.
(See NATIONAL AFFAIRS)

Number 1

Circulation Office, 350 East 22nd Street, Chicago.　(Reg. U. S. Pat. Off.)　Editorial and Advertising Offices, 135 East 42nd Street, New York.

3

ALPHABET SOUP

"**W**ill he make good in the White House? The country is only too ready to hope so," opined the editors at *Time* in the January 2, 1933, cover story on FDR, the magazine's Man of the Year.

Had Giuseppe Zangara been an ace assassin, FDR would have been Dead Man of the Year.

Date: February 15, 1933.

Place: Bayfront Park in Miami, Florida.

FDR had just given a brief speech from atop the backseat of a Buick convertible when Zangara, a hapless, jobless thirty-two-year-old bricklayer, aimed a .32-caliber revolver at the president-elect's head. He got off five shots before bystanders were on him.

Chicago's mayor, Anton Cermak, was one of several people Zangara wounded. The mayor had been standing by FDR's car when the shooting started.

Giuseppe Zangara at Florida's Raiford Prison.

As for FDR, he was A-OK and later as buoyant as always before the press and the public. Unperturbed, even fearless, he seemed.

Zangara seemed fearless, too—and disturbed—when arraigned. "When I am living I try to kill president because capitalists kill me. Take all my life away. I am no good. Stomach like drunk man." Originally sentenced to eighty years in the Big House, Zangara got the electric chair after Mayor Cermak died.

Few wept for Zangara. He had murdered a mayor and tried to off the president-elect, after all. Plus, as always happens in hard times, hatred for foreigners, along with various shameful -*isms,* was on the rise.

As for Zangara, he was zany until the very end. Strapped into Old Sparky, he cried out, "*Viva Italia!* Good-bye to all poor people everywhere!" He then told his executioner, "Pusha da button! Go ahead, pusha da button!"

Date: March 20, 1933.

By then, FDR was officially the nation's thirty-second president.

<blockquote>
The lobby of The First-Central Trust Company was a madhouse. Bewildered grocery store owners and frantic housewives stood in line with their passbooks shrilly demanding their money.

—Journalist Ruth McKenney, remembering February 27, 1933, in Akron, Ohio.
</blockquote>

Back on Saturday, March 4, Inauguration Day, FDR's confidence seemed in overdrive, beneath a brooding sky: "This great Nation will endure as it has endured, will revive and will prosper. So, first of all, let me assert my firm belief that the only thing we have to fear is fear itself."

Fear was real among the hundred thousand people crowded around the Capitol and among millions near radios.

Even more people were out of work. More former full-time workers were part-timers now. Several municipalities were too broke to pay teachers and civil servants, including cops. About 40 percent of homeowners were behind on their mortgages. On average, about one thousand homes were falling into foreclosure every day.

Hordes of people with surplus cash had been stocking up on canned goods and other staples. Some of these same people had stampeded banks, convinced that their money would be safer stuffed in socks, crammed under floorboards, or tucked into other hiding places. Since January, depositors had withdrawn several hundred million dollars in currency and gold. Another four thousand banks had gone bust.

Yes, people were afraid, very afraid, but there stood FDR insisting, "The only thing we have to fear is fear itself— nameless, unreasoning, unjustified terror which paralyzes needed efforts to convert retreat into advance."

One key to that advance: putting people before profits. FDR signaled that the Three Bs were in for a chastening. Also, he understood the need for speed: "This Nation asks for action, and action now."

For major action, the president would need to work with the legislative branch, but the new Congress wasn't due to convene for many months—not until December 4 (another holdover from the horse-and-buggy days).

FDR couldn't—wouldn't—wait. He announced that he would call Congress into special session.

Democrats now controlled Congress. On FDR's coattails, they had picked up ninety seats in the House (for a total of 310 of 432 seats) and thirteen in the Senate (for 60 of 96 seats). Chances were that Congress would rapidly pass bills that the president favored and helped form. Nevertheless, FDR announced that if Congress dillydallied, he would get drastic: "I shall ask the Congress for the one remaining instrument to meet the crisis—broad Executive power to wage a war against the emergency, as great as the power that would be given to me if we were in fact invaded by a foreign foe."

People cheered.

The man had just said that if he saw fit, he would make a grab for absolute power—

People cheered?

Powers to the Prez

In addition to using the powers that the Constitution gives the POTUS (president of the United States), such as appointments to the SCOTUS (Supreme Court of the United States), a president can shape and make policy in a number of ways. Two are:

- **Presidential proclamation:** A decree to the public at large. Some presidential proclamations are merely symbolic and of little consequence (hypothetical example: National Save Your Pennies Day). Others are quite consequential (historical example: the Emancipation Proclamation).

- **EO (executive order):** A decree to the government, ostensibly in the furtherance of a law or a power already vested in the president by that law or the Constitution.

> **Of course we all realize that dictatorships and even semi-dictatorships in peace time are quite contrary to the spirit of American institutions. . . . And yet—well, a genial and lighthearted dictator might be a relief.**
>
> —February 13, 1933: *Barron's* magazine.

It was when Italy hit rock bottom, in 1922, that the fascist dictator Benito Mussolini—Il Duce ("the leader")—began his rule. More recently, in January 1933, Adolf Hitler had become chancellor of a hard-up Germany and would soon be the führer. How strong a leader did those cheering Americans want?

FDR was all action during his first weekend in office, conferring with cabinet members, members of Congress, governors, bankers, and other power brokers. What's more, he issued two presidential proclamations.

The first called Congress back to work on Thursday.

The second declared a national "bank holiday," a euphemism for a shutdown.

March 4, 1933—Inauguration Day.

WHOA!

From the March 16, 1933, *Courier-Post* of Camden, New Jersey. The man in the portrait looking on in apparent approval is the past POTUS (1901–1909) Teddy Roosevelt, FDR's fifth cousin and ER's uncle. While campaigning in 1903, this Republican had promised Americans a "square deal."

Without the president's say-so, no banking institutions could do any business for several days, until Thursday, March 9. Withdrawals, deposits, redeeming dollars for gold—all this and more, verboten.

The point of this proclamation: (1) to stop runs on banks, and (2) to prevent U.S. gold reserves from dwindling by keeping individuals and businesses from redeeming their dollars for gold. America was on the gold standard. No gold, no money.

When FDR issued the proclamation on banking, many people were already having a cash-flow problem because most banks were already on "holiday" by a governor's or bank president's decree. Until the national bank holiday was over, people not on the bum but lacking a stash of cash would resort to bartering, dropping IOUs, raiding their kids' piggy banks, and asking brothers, sisters, and others if they could spare a dime.

On Thursday, March 9, high noon, Congress was back in session—day one of what became FDR's famous First Hundred Days of action! action! action!

New rules.

New regulations.

New deals through a slew of new agencies.

SOME MAJOR ACTIONS DURING
THE FIRST HUNDRED DAYS

Here and throughout, the date of a piece of legislation is the date of its passage in Congress. FDR often signed a bill into law the very same day.

MARCH
9
Thursday

Emergency Banking Act has as its goal to prevent the total collapse of banks. Rescue measures include:

- Ratifying FDR's "bank holiday"; empowering him to extend it if he sees fit—which he does (new end date: March 13); and making him boss of the financial system.

- Calling for Treasury to scrutinize banks' assets and balance sheets. Financially sound banks will receive a fast stamp of approval to reopen. Shaky ones will be restructured, starting with new management. Banks in terrible shape (where money they owe far exceeds the money they are owed) will be closed.

- Enabling the RFC, created during the Hoover administration, to bail out troubled but viable banks with an infusion of cash in several ways, including by buying their stock and making secured loans.

MARCH
20
Monday

National Economy Act reduces government spending by $500 million (31%). It does this by cutting some agencies and slashing salaries of federal employees—including members of Congress and the president—by 15% and slicing some veterans' benefits. Goal: a balanced budget, another of FDR's campaign promises.

MARCH
31
Friday

Reforestation Relief Act paves the way for the **CCC** (Civilian Conservation Corps), designed to put single young men (late teens to early twenties) from hard-up families to work on the nation's great outdoors, chiefly forests and national parks. Pay: $30 a month on average, with about 90% of the money sent straight to the young men's families. Foresters will be in charge of training. Army reserve officers will run the camps in which the young men will live. The CCC's goal: to beautify the nation, reduce hooliganism, and get money to the needy.

APRIL
5
Wednesday

With **EO 6102,** FDR decrees that Americans can own only up to $100 worth of gold. Exceptions include gold teeth, rare coins, and certain jewelry. People have until May 1 to surrender their gold to Treasury (via designated banks). In return, they'll get $20.67 per troy ounce. Penalty for noncompliance: a fine up to $10,000 or imprisonment up to ten years. Goal: to stop a run on gold and increase Uncle Sam's stockpile of it.

MAY
12
Friday

Federal Emergency Relief Act leads to **FERA** (Federal Emergency Relief Administration). Immediate goal: to funnel money—$500 million—to states for direct relief (such as money and food) and work relief (jobs). Ultimate goal: to keep people from starving, stealing, and going off.

Agricultural Adjustment Act creates the **AAA** (Agricultural Adjustment Administration), aka the Triple A. Through the AAA, Uncle Sam will pay farmers to cut production of cotton, corn, pork, and other key commodities. Some crops already in the ground will have to be plowed up and destroyed. Excess hogs and piglets—slaughtered. Goal: to raise farm prices by lowering farm production—to get supply more in sync with demand. The money to subsidize farmers will come from a "processing" tax. Example: a tax on cotton when spun, on corn when milled, on livestock when slaughtered.

Tacked onto the AAA act is a rider that empowers the president to stimulate inflation in a number of ways, including ordering the Fed to buy up to $3 billion in government bonds; adjusting the gold-to-greenback ratio; and ordering Treasury to print up to $3 billion in greenbacks.

Emergency Farm Mortgage Act establishes a loan fund of $200 million for farmers facing foreclosure.

MAY
18
Thursday

Tennessee Valley Authority Act leads to the **TVA** (Tennessee Valley Authority). Goal: to develop the Tennessee Valley region by, among other things, building dams and power plants in this economically depressed seven-state region.

MAY
27
Saturday

Securities Act of 1933 (aka **Truth in Securities Act**) compels companies issuing new stocks and bonds to register with the government and provide complete information on their financial shape. The act also puts in place a system by which swindlers can be sued. Overarching goal: to restore confidence in the financial markets.

JUNE
5
Monday

A congressional joint resolution signed by FDR abolishes gold contracts. No longer can one party agree to pay another party in gold. Goal: to tie up a loose end to EO 6102. People can't very well carry out a contract for payment in gold when it is unlawful to possess any significant amount of gold. The resolution is the final nail in the coffin for the ability of ordinary people and businesses to own a significant amount of gold and deal in gold legally.

JUNE
13
Tuesday

Home Owners' Refinancing Act begets **HOLC** (Home Owners' Loan Corporation) to offer people a chance to redo their mortgages. Nonfarm homes valued at under $20,000 can get a new mortgage at a lower interest rate (5% versus 8% or higher) and for a longer period of time (roughly twenty years versus the typical five years).

JUNE
16
Friday

Another banking act, best known as the **Glass-Steagall Act of 1933,** after the two politicians who sponsored it: Senator Carter Glass (D-VA), father of the Federal Reserve System and a former secretary of the treasury, and Representative Henry Steagall (D-AL). The most consequential facets of the Glass-Steagall Act mandates are:

• Banks must choose: be a commercial bank or an investment bank. No more being both. Goal: to put an end to commercial banks engaging in crazy speculation with their customers' deposits and underwriting all kinds of securities. Exception: government bonds.

• Creation of the **FDIC** (Federal Deposit Insurance Corporation), a temporary entity, to insure that if a bank fails, depositors won't lose all their money. Participating banks will fund the insurance by paying annual premiums. The FDIC will be effective January 1, 1934. Amount to be covered: $2,500 (equivalent to about $100,000 today).

Farm Credit Act yields the **FCS** (Farm Credit System) to make it easier for farmers to get low-interest loans for their sowing and reaping needs.

National Industrial Recovery Act (NIRA) nets two new deals:

• **NRA** (National Recovery Administration). Goal: to strengthen the industrial sector of the economy. With government oversight—and presidential final say—industries (from coal to cotton) must come up with codes of fair play regarding such things as hours, wages, and retail prices, and in so doing end cutthroat competition that can drag everybody down. Example: businesses that slashed prices often maintained their profit margin by cutting wages. The act's **Section 7(a)** says that workers have a right to unionize and to bargain collectively (to set up negotiations between representatives of employers and employees).

• **PWA** (Public Works Administration). Goal: job creation. The PWA will oversee and fund state-sponsored capital improvement projects, such as the construction of bridges, tunnels, and water and sewage systems. Budget: $3.3 billion, with $125 million earmarked for low-income housing.

From the March 11, 1933,
Pittsburgh Press.

"This is Chapter 1—in epitome—of the Roosevelt regime. And what a chapter! What a régime!" wrote J. Frederick Essary in "The New Deal for Nearly Four Months."

Essary's article ran in the *Literary Digest* a few weeks after Congress adjourned on June 16, the finale of the First Hundred Days.

"Fifteen weeks have elapsed since the New Dealers began dealing," Essary reminded readers. "Fifteen weeks of high-pressure activity. Fifteen weeks of whirlwind changes in the old order, of experimental panaceas, of legislative novelties and of practically unchallenged Executive domination of the colossal organism which we call the Federal Government."

During all that action, FDR had talked to the nation about the whirlwind changes.

"The president wants to come into your home and sit at your fireside for a little fireside chat," said CBS radio announcer Robert Trout in his setup piece on Sunday night, March 12, 1933, the day before the first wave of banks were to reopen.

In this fireside chat, FDR talked about how banks operate (only keeping a fraction of deposits on hand and investing most of the money) and one reason banks fail (a rush of withdrawals). FDR also told the nation what the government was doing to make the banking system rock solid. "Confidence and courage are the essentials of success in carrying out our plan," he said. "You people must have faith; you must not be stampeded by rumors or guesses. Let us unite in banishing fear. . . . Together we cannot fail."

When banks began opening on Monday, March 13, there were more deposits than withdrawals. Often, when FDR felt that the nation needed reassuring—or convincing—he would have a fireside chat.

FDR wasn't the first president to address the nation on the radio, but he pioneered in being a great communicator (and manipulator) through this medium. Along with a winning voice, he had an amazing ability to discuss public policy without talking down to people. His warm, conversational style became the gold standard for future presidents.

FDR's second fireside chat came on May 7, 1933. Goal: to inspire confidence in more of the action taken thus far, such as the creation of the CCC.

The president didn't give another fireside chat until July 24, 1933, five weeks after Congress adjourned.

Why so long?

"First, I think that we all wanted the opportunity of a little quiet thought to examine and assimilate in a mental picture the crowding events of the hundred days which had been devoted to the starting of the wheels of the New Deal." Second, wheels need hubs, axles, spokes—it takes time to get things rolling. (One example of forward motion: the CCC already had over 250,000 enrollees.)

The real goal of FDR's July fireside chat was to rally support for the AAA and the NRA: "For many years the two great barriers to a normal prosperity have been low farm prices and

❝ Of course, it is entirely out of the ordinary to pass legislation . . . not even in print at the time it is offered. . . . The house is burning down and the president of the United States says this is the way to put out the fire. And to me at this time, there is only one answer to that question and that is to give the president what he demands and says is necessary to meet the situation. ❞

—March 9, 1932: Representative Bertrand Snell (R-NY) on the emergency banking bill.

March 12, 1933: FDR giving his first fireside chat. "I tried to picture a mason at work on a new building, a girl behind a counter, a farmer in his field," he later said of his chats.

By 1933, more than half of U.S. households had at least one radio. This Philco tabletop Baby Grand Cathedral was a very popular pick.

the creeping paralysis of unemployment. These factors have cut the purchasing power of the country in half."

Speaking of the AAA, FDR said: "Without our help the farmers cannot get together and cut production, and the Farm Bill gives them a method of bringing their production down to a reasonable level and of obtaining reasonable prices for their crops."

Higher wholesale prices would inevitably lead to higher retail prices—inflation. Who in the world wanted to see, say, their grocery bill go up?

FDR anticipated that reaction and tried to get people to imagine a rising tide lifting all boats. "It is obvious that if we can greatly increase the purchasing power of the tens of millions of our people who make a living from farming and the distribution of farm crops, we shall greatly increase the consumption of those goods which are turned out by industry." In other words, the more farmers earned, the more they could spend at dry-goods stores and mail-order firms such as Sears, Roebuck. The more farmers bought, the more merchants would purchase from their suppliers. This demand-supply dynamic would, in theory, aid recovery.

Inflation without economic growth: bad.

Inflation with economic growth: good.

FDR made a similar argument when boosting the NRA: "If all employers in each competitive group agree to pay their workers the same wages—reasonable wages—and require the same hours—reasonable hours—then higher wages and shorter hours will hurt no employer" and ultimately help employers in a range of industries. As employment and wages rose, so would consumption.

The president urged businesses to get with the program. By then, the NRA had a "blanket code," ground rules that FDR issued a few days after he signed the act that created the agency.

For one, this blanket code banned full-time wage work for girls and boys under sixteen in many workplaces. Its twofold goal: to reduce exploitation of children and to free up jobs for adults.

FDR's blanket code also established maximum weekly hours for blue-collar and white-collar workers (generally, thirty-five to forty hours), both to spread around the number of available jobs and to prevent these workers from having to pull ten- or twelve-hour days. Also part of the package: a minimum wage of $12 to $15 a week.

To goad businesses into going along with the blanket code, the president announced that those who did would receive "a badge of honor"—a sign announcing "We Do Our Part"—to proudly display.

FDR wanted employers and employees to cooperate in good faith. That was the goal of Section 7(a): to encourage labor and capital to relate to each other as partners, not adversaries.

Some Economic -Ations

- **Deflation:** A drop in the prices of goods and services, often triggered by a drop in spending, and leading to job losses. Also, a decrease of the money supply.

- **Inflation:** A rise in the prices of goods and services, usually without a fully equivalent rise in wages. Also, an increase in the money supply.

- **Hyperinflation:** Runaway inflation.

- **Reflation:** Monetary policies a government employs to stop deflation and stimulate the economy. Also, getting more money into circulation.

- **Stagnation:** Lack of, or very slow, economic growth, accompanied by rising unemployment.

- **Stagflation:** Stagnation plus inflation.

While labor and capital were acting in good faith, the president hoped they'd also keep the faith that recovery was possible. Still, he confessed, "I have no faith in 'cure-alls' but I believe that we can greatly influence economic forces."

Harry Hopkins was one of the New Deal fast and furious forces in D.C. This native of Sioux City, Iowa, with a passion for racetrack action had worked in the social service sector for years. That career included serving as an administrator at New York City's AICP (Association for Improving the Condition of the Poor) and, years later, as chief of TERA. Now he was in charge of FERA. Before he even had a proper office, hasty Hopkins dispatched to states about $5 million of his $500 million budget for relief.

FDR's pick for secretary of the interior was another Harry: lawyer Harold Ickes, former head of the Chicago branch of the NAACP (National Association for the Advancement of Colored People).

One of Ickes's jobs as secretary of the interior was to manage the PWA. As he reviewed proposals for bridges and other behemoth public works, nitpicky Ickes was determined to keep the PWA corruption-free.

FDR's secretary of labor was determined to see that workers, especially, got a better deal. She was Massachusetts native Frances Perkins, America's first woman to hold a cabinet post—and the target of nonsense and nastiness from both men and women who believed that a woman had no business being anything but a wife and mother (and Perkins was both), let alone the head of a major government department.

Knowing she'd catch hell, Perkins still said yes when FDR asked her to take the job back in February 1933—and it was a yes on her terms. "I don't want to say yes to you unless you know what I'd like to do and are willing to have me go ahead and try," said Perkins to FDR. She then ticked off her list. It in-

December 1933: FDR with his first cabinet. *Left to right:* Daniel Roper, secretary of commerce; Harold Ickes, secretary of the interior; James Farley, postmaster general; George Dern, secretary of war; Cordell Hull, secretary of state; FDR; William Woodin, secretary of the treasury; Homer Cummings, attorney general; Claude Swanson, secretary of the navy; Henry Wallace, secretary of agriculture; and Frances Perkins, secretary of labor.

cluded establishing maximum hours and minimum wages for workers, and a safety net for those who lost their jobs through no fault of their own. She also wanted child labor verboten.

Perkins's passion for workers' welfare was not news to FDR. When he was New York's governor, she had served as the state's industrial commissioner (head of its department of labor). Before that, including when Perkins and FDR's mutual mentor, Al Smith, was governor, she had held several posts with agencies that scoped out wretched working conditions. One was chief of the Committee on Safety of the City of New York, created in response to the March 25, 1911, conflagration that erupted in a Greenwich Village firetrap: the Triangle Shirtwaist Company.

Perkins was nearby, at a friend's home, when fire bells sounded. Once on the scene, she saw desperate souls leaping from windows and burned bodies pile up in the street. The fire, in which close to 150 people died, most of them young immigrant women, made Perkins even more of a zealot for the laboring class.

"Yes," said FDR after Perkins ran down her list, "I'll back you."

Once on the job, Perkins worked on legislation that led to the CCC, FERA, NRA, PWA, and other new deals of the First Hundred Days, checking quite a few things off her list.

The First Lady was an equally important New Dealer. ER had frowned upon the CCC's being for guys only and was the godmother of residential work camps for gals from broke and hungry families. New York's Bear Mountain was the site of the first such program, which some in the press derided as the "She, She, She."

For years, ER had served as her husband's "legs" during campaigns. So now it was nothing for her to travel around the country—by car, by train, by plane—to bear witness to people's plights and take the pulse of the New Deal.

ER let people know in print as well as in person that she cared. "I Want You to Write to Me" was the title of her article in the August 1933 *Woman's Home Companion.* "I want you to tell me about the particular problems which puzzle or sadden you, but I also want you to write me about what has brought joy into your life, and how you are adjusting yourself to the new conditions in this amazing changing world."

She promised to respect people's privacy: "Your confidence will not be betrayed. Your name will not be printed unless you give permission." ER closed simply with, "I want you to write to me."

People needed no prompting. After the inauguration, FDR

June 1933: ER in L.A.

and ER had received nearly half a million letters and telegrams, many of them from ordinary folks, sharing their needs, expressing their hopes. After the First Hundred Days, there was even more mail. (ER alone would receive some three hundred thousand letters by the end of 1933.)

FDR proved true to his word about being willing to switch up if something he tried didn't work out. Take that AAA-spawned business of plowing up crops and slaughtering livestock. People went nuts. So, in October 1933, FDR issued an EO creating the FSRC (Federal Surplus Relief Corporation). Goal: to buy surplus farm produce and distribute it to agencies and organizations helping the broke and hungry, including FERA. Besides funding state relief efforts, FERA was

1933: Members of FDR's Tree Army, as the CCC was called. These two are surveying an area of South Dakota's Black Hills. Others would tackle soil erosion and flood control, among other things. They wouldn't all be young men. For one, after World War I vets cried foul about the age limit, FDR allowed many of them to join the corps.

evolving into a full-fledged social service agency, operating food pantries, transient camps, and more.

By late 1933, millions were still in crisis. Winter would be wicked for so many. At Harry Hopkins's urging, FDR created (by EO) a temporary work relief program, the CWA (Civil Works Administration). Goal: to put people to work on shovel-ready improvement projects, like painting public buildings. Though created with some PWA funds, the CWA was a division of Hopkins's FERA.

Quipped scrappy Al Smith of all these agencies: "It looks as though one of the absent-minded professors had played anagrams with the alphabet soup."

FDR and Smith were now foes. The rift began when both men sought to be their party's nominee in 1932, but Smith's alphabet soup remark was no matter of mere jealousy. He was a stalwart of the Democratic Party's pro-business wing. FDR had snubbed that gang by not offering Smith or his allies plum posts in the administration.

From the 1928 campaign, when poor-born Smith made history as the first Irish Catholic major-party presidential candidate.

One thing Smith and FDR agreed on was that national Prohibition had to go, and it did.

Back in February, a twenty-first amendment to the Constitution calling for Prohibition's repeal had passed in Congress. While the amendment was out to the states for ratification, Congress ended the ban on beverages containing up to 3.2 percent alcohol (the Beer and Wine Revenue Act). Within a week, Uncle Sam was looking at about $4 million in revenue from taxes on booze.

The government could look forward to millions more after December 5, 1933. That was the day that the Twenty-first Amendment became law, approved by the needed 75 percent of the states.

Some people were convinced that happy days were on the horizon.

Others were calling for FDR's head.

> 66 **Will you please investigate the various relief agencies in many cities of the United States. The cities where there are a large foreign and jewish population. No wonder the cities are now on the verge of bankruptcy because we are feeding a lot of ignorant foreigners by giving them relief. . . . I would suggest to deport all foreigners and jews who are not citizens.** 99
>
> —October 1933: To Harry Hopkins from a New Yorker and signed "A Taxpayer."

1934: Some of the 6,000 men at work on a CWA project in San Francisco.

4

IS ROOSEVELT GOING SOCIALIST?

"**N**ineteen hundred and thirty-four will see the crisis in the New Deal," began Jay Franklin's article in the March 10, 1934, *Liberty* magazine.

"Is Roosevelt Going Socialist?" the title teased.

Jay Franklin didn't think so, but he knew that this was the charge from the Right.

"For several months there has been a rising chorus of criticism directed against Roosevelt's 'radicalism' and against the 'socialism' of the New Deal."

And there was more. There were shouts and murmurs that FDR was a dupe. "The theory has been widely spread that a small group of secret revolutionaries in the government have conspired to commit the President to policies which will lead him, without his knowledge and against his will, toward the creation of a socialistic commonwealth."

Circa 1935: Rexford Guy Tugwell.

Those alleged "secret revolutionaries" were members of the president's "brain trust," as people came to call the policy wonks/sounding boards FDR had gathered around him when he set his sights on the White House.

Chief among the brain trusters were three professors at New York City's Columbia University: Ray Moley (public law), Adolf Berle Jr. (corporation law), and Rex Tugwell (economics). The three didn't agree on everything, but the consensus was that capitalism needed some boundaries.

Rex Tugwell, the most radical of the bunch, thought something needed to be done about the concentration of wealth. He also believed that agriculture and the well-being of farmers was critical to economic recovery. Tugwell, whom FDR made assistant secretary of agriculture, was a co-architect of the AAA.

While FDR embraced many of the brain trusters' ideas, he also rejected plenty. He was nobody's puppet. The notion that he could be hoodwinked into socialism was ludicrous, but it was an effective scare tactic by people furious over the federal government getting so big.

And FDR so powerful.

And spending so much money.

Gone was the president's commitment to a balanced budget. He had decided that it was more important to get people *un*broke and *un*hungry than it was for Uncle Sam to be in the black. To this end, he got on board with deficit spending: when the government commits to more outgo than projected income from taxes within a fiscal year.

Most of the New Deal's critics on the Right had applauded the bailout of banks but felt that Joe and Jane Q. Public simply had to tough it out. Many opponents of big government spending could still afford ritzy cars and caviar. Others were middle-income folks who could never imagine themselves between a rock and a hard place.

Anti–New Dealers were always on the lookout for opportunities to ridicule the alphabet soup. Take the CWA, discontinued in the spring of 1934. Its workers did much that needed doing, from building two hundred thousand miles' worth of roads to building or fixing up four thousand schools. Yet, many conservatives zeroed in on those few projects, like raking leaves, that most everyone saw as wasteful spending.

Unless you were the souls working those rakes: people who had been surviving on slumgullion stew, people supremely grateful for work. When given a choice between the dole (direct relief) and work relief, most able-bodied people preferred the job, even if it was busywork.

Getting on the dole was often a humiliating experience. Some caseworkers treated the needy like dirt. In some places, the amount of relief was based on race, with nonwhites receiving less than whites did, whether it was cash, boxes of groceries, or vouchers for food, fuel, and medicine. Political affiliation was sometimes a factor in who got what and how much.

❝ There was something strange about these poor people: Nearly all of them, especially the old people, came in apparently terribly frightened. . . . I could actually see them shake.❞

—1938: Louise Armstrong, director of a FERA office in Michigan.

A window sticker in support of the National Recovery Administration.

Early on, the NRA had a great deal of support from most folks, thanks to the NRA chief—the boozing, bodacious, bullying General Hugh "Iron Pants" Johnson. He came up with the NRA symbol, the Blue Eagle: a cocky-looking thunderbird gripping a cog in one talon and lightning bolts in the other.

There were Blue Eagle posters and placards, banners and buttons. There were Blue Eagle rallies and Blue Eagle parades. There was a lot of Blue Eagle pressure: for employers to sign on and for consumers to boycott those who did not.

"State socialism." That's what media mogul William Randolph Hearst called the NRA. The letters really stood for "No Recovery Allowed," Hearst said. (In the black community, "NRA" stood for "Negro Run Around" and "Negroes Ruined Again," among other things, because the agency sanctioned blacks getting paid less than whites for the same work.)

For many employers the worst part of all was Section 7(a) of the act that created the NRA. Section 7(a) made labor roar.

"THE PRESIDENT WANTS *YOU* TO ORGANIZE!" That's how labor spun Section 7(a). This slogan appeared on placards and on the sides of union organizers' cars and trucks blazing around on recruitment drives. Union membership jumped.

Even before Section 7(a), unions were growing. Take the ILGWU (International Ladies' Garment Workers' Union). By

The NIRA's Section 7(a)

"Every code of fair competition, agreement, and license approved, prescribed, or issued under this title shall contain the following conditions: (1) That employees shall have the right to organize and bargain collectively through representatives of their own choosing, and shall be free from the interference, restraint, or coercion of employers of labor, or their agents, in the designation of such representatives or in self-organization or in other concerted activities for the purpose of collective bargaining or other mutual aid or protection; (2) that no employee and no one seeking employment shall be required as a condition of employment to join any company union or to refrain from joining, organizing, or assisting a labor organization of his own choosing; and (3) that employers shall comply with the maximum hours of labor, minimum rates of pay, and other conditions of employment, approved or prescribed by the President."

the spring of 1934, its membership had soared to two hundred thousand from forty thousand in 1932.

ILGWU was one of the few industrial unions in the umbrella labor organization the AFL (American Federation of Labor). Its logo: the handshake. Its motto: *Labor Omnia Vincit* (Latin for "Labor [or Work] Conquers All").

When the AFL formed back in the 1880s, the only unions that could affiliate with it were all-male, all-white, and organized along a particular craft or skill (like carpentry). In contrast, an industrial union had skilled, semiskilled, and unskilled workers in the same field standing shoulder to shoulder.

The UMW (United Mine Workers of America) was another industrial union in the AFL fold—and the largest in the nation. The UMW's powerhouse of a president, John Lewis, was pressing the AFL to embrace industrial unionism and aggressively organize among the millions of as yet un-unionized semiskilled and unskilled workers—and without prejudice. After all, thanks to technology, demand for skilled workers

District 1 covered eastern Pennsylvania.

UMW chief John Llewellyn Lewis, former coal miner and son of a coal miner, during a November 1935 address.

43

was dropping, and demand for "machine tenders" was rising. Lewis was past impatient with the AFL's failure to recognize that the more unity, the more strength.

Workers would need strength. Many business owners gave Section 7(a) the brush-off and ignored NRA codes on wages and hours. They got away with this by firing workers who complained, siccing hired thugs on union activists, and bribing or bullying NRA officials to look the other way.

Contrary to union propaganda, FDR wasn't particularly pro-union. Yes, he wanted workers to get a fair deal, but he

Circa 1934.

This issue of the *Literary Digest* reported the results of the magazine's poll on FDR's policies. Approval rating: 61%.

The New Deal The Issue

wanted management to *give* it, not workers to *take* it. Back in 1933, by EO, FDR had created the NLB (National Labor Board) to mediate conflicts between labor and management. To head the NLB, he tapped Senator Robert Wagner (D-NY), whose New Deal credentials included helping to draft bills that created the NRA and FERA.

Along with his friend Frances Perkins, Wagner was among the most ardent pro-labor public servants. Problem was while the NLB could mediate, it couldn't make management do anything. Its only big stick for ornery employers was to urge NRA chief Hugh Johnson to take away their Blue Eagle.

When mediation didn't work, workers had their age-old cudgel: *STRIKE!*

More than a million workers joined in a total of roughly sixteen hundred strikes back in 1933. Result: some workers received better wages and shorter hours, along with recognition of their unions.

Business blamed FDR for labor's moxie. As that chorus of

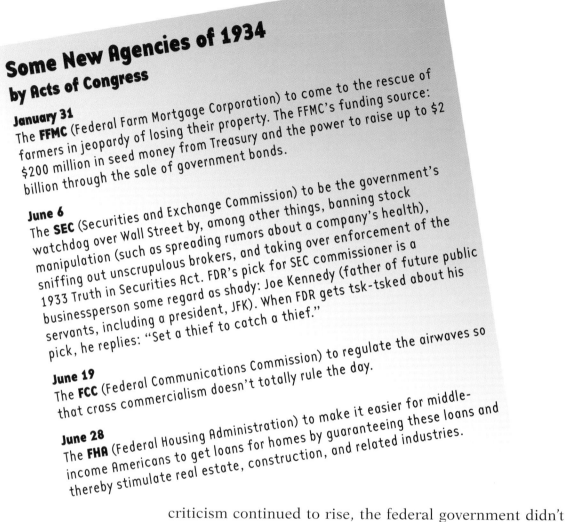

Some New Agencies of 1934
by Acts of Congress

January 31
The **FFMC** (Federal Farm Mortgage Corporation) to come to the rescue of farmers in jeopardy of losing their property. The FFMC's funding source: $200 million in seed money from Treasury and the power to raise up to $2 billion through the sale of government bonds.

June 6
The **SEC** (Securities and Exchange Commission) to be the government's watchdog over Wall Street by, among other things, banning stock manipulation (such as spreading rumors about a company's health), sniffing out unscrupulous brokers, and taking over enforcement of the 1933 Truth in Securities Act. FDR's pick for SEC commissioner is a businessperson some regard as shady: Joe Kennedy (father of future public servants, including a president, JFK). When FDR gets tsk-tsked about his pick, he replies: "Set a thief to catch a thief."

June 19
The **FCC** (Federal Communications Commission) to regulate the airwaves so that crass commercialism doesn't totally rule the day.

June 28
The **FHA** (Federal Housing Administration) to make it easier for middle-income Americans to get loans for homes by guaranteeing these loans and thereby stimulate real estate, construction, and related industries.

criticism continued to rise, the federal government didn't get shy.

It got bigger.

The federal government's growth didn't stop with additions to the alphabet soup.

For one, Congress okayed another $950 million for direct and work relief. There was also more news on gold: the Gold Reserve Act made the Fed hand over to Treasury all its gold (in exchange for gold certificates). Now the federal government had a lock on the nation's gold.

Added to that, with an EO, FDR declared that one troy ounce was no longer worth $20.67 but $35. By doing this, he increased the amount of money Treasury could produce. That hypothetical one million troy ounces of gold that once allowed $51,675,000 in circulation now allowed $87,500,000. (Not until 1971 did the nation truly abandon the gold standard. That's when it switched to fiat money: legal tender with no intrinsic value.)

Farmers still drowning in debt caught a break thanks to a bill sponsored by Senator Lynn Frazier and Representative William Lemke, both from North Dakota. Now if farmers so petitioned federal courts, judges could slash their debt relative to the current value of their property (and the value of most property had fallen). The courts could also grant farmers one heck of a breathing spell to pay off the remaining debt: five years. What's more, farmers already in foreclosure but still on the farm could stay put and take up to five years to get their property out of hock. (While farmers felt relieved, some of their creditors felt robbed.)

Other farm aid included a law adding beef, barley, and other products to the list of AAA-controlled commodities. Another law increased the money pot, by $40 million, from which farmers could borrow for sowing and reaping needs.

Meanwhile, nature had another blow in store for folks in prairie states. In May, there came another dust storm, with several million tons of earth blowing away, some of it touching down as far away as Boston.

More American dreams became dust in the wind. More people in Oklahoma, Arkansas, and other Dust Bowl states would pack up and head to the West Coast. For FERA, the natural disaster meant more rescue work to do in the afflicted area and along the migration trail.

Treasury Versus the Fed

- **Treasury (U.S. Department of the Treasury)** manages the government's money, from collecting what's due (such as taxes) to making good on its IOUs. Treasury also produces paper money through the BEP (Bureau of Engraving and Printing) and coins through the U.S. Mint.

- **The Fed (Federal Reserve System),** as the nation's central bank, is the banker (and the boss) of banks and other financial institutions, as well as Treasury's banker. The Fed maintains Treasury's checking account, distributes to financial institutions the currency and coin Treasury creates, and handles the buying and selling of savings bonds and other government securities. The Fed also manages the nation's monetary policy (all things pertaining to the money supply). This includes controlling the cost of credit (interest rates). When the Fed thinks the economy is overheating, it might deter borrowing by raising interest rates. When the Fed thinks the economy needs stimulating, it might lower interest rates. (The cheaper it is to borrow money, the more likely people are to take out loans for homes, business expansion, and other things.)

ONE OF SOUTH DAKOTA'S "BLACK BLIZZARDS" 1934

Dust storms would plague the nation for several years to come.

On the evening of June 28, 1934, the day Congress adjourned, FDR had a fireside chat. In it, he talked about the essence of the New Deal: the Four Rs.

There was *relief:* "because the primary concern of any Government dominated by the humane ideals of democracy is the simple principle that in a land of vast resources no one should be permitted to starve." Thus, FERA.

The NRA and the AAA represented *recovery* measures. As for new regulations, as well as monetary and fiscal policies, they represented the need for *reform* and *reconstruction:* "reform because much of our trouble today and in the past few years has been due to a lack of understanding of the elementary principles of justice and fairness by those in whom leadership in business and finance was placed—reconstruction because new conditions in our economic life as well as old but neglected conditions had to be corrected."

FDR also addressed his critics in this chat: "A few timid people, who fear progress, will try to give you new and strange names for what we are doing. Sometimes they will call it 'Fascism,' sometimes 'Communism,' sometimes 'Regimentation,' sometimes 'Socialism.' But, in so doing, they are trying to make very complex and theoretical something that is really very simple and very practical." He then likened the nation to the White House.

During FDR's summer vacation, the part of the White House reserved as the president's office space was going to get a makeover. The work would include new plumbing, rewiring, expansion of the ground floor, and the construction of a second story. Result: the West Wing.

"The structural lines of the old Executive office building will remain," FDR explained. "If I were to listen to the arguments of some prophets of calamity who are talking these days, I should . . . fear that while I am away for a few weeks the architects might build some strange new Gothic tower or a factory building or perhaps a replica of the Kremlin or of the Potsdam Palace. But I have no such fears."

Relax, said the president. *America, like the White House, is being renovated, not demolished.*

A symbol of reform: The FDIC's first seal for participating banks to display.

From a deck of souvenir playing cards.

FDR was looking forward to some R & R on the seas and in Hawaii that summer, while others in the money would be on safaris in Africa, on cruises around the world, or at their getaway homes in places like Bar Harbor and Palm Beach.

Thousands of hoity-toity and hoi-polloi types alike would crowd the Windy City for season two of the world's fair, with its manifold exhibits, from the Skyride to the bizarro-world attractions at the Odditorium, hosted by Ripley's Believe It or Not.

When Boris Karloff and Bela Lugosi co-starred in this 1934 film, they were already horror genre hits as Frankenstein's monster and Count Dracula, respectively.

People would also spice up their summer with baseball games and barbecues, picnics and prizefights. Some would hit nightclubs or sit by a radio to savor the sounds of Duke Ellington, Benny Goodman, and other kings of swing. Still others would spend lemonade days with bestsellers like Pearl S. Buck's *The Good Earth* or Hervey Allen's *Anthony Adverse* or perhaps F. Scott Fitzgerald's commercial flop *Tender Is the Night.*

For two bits or less, you could escape into one of Shirley Temple's feel-good flicks, or maybe horror, on the order of *The Black Cat;* adventure, such as *Treasure Island;* or a screwball comedy like Frank Capra's *It Happened One Night.*

If you had a hankering for gangster films that glorified criminals and amplified violence, the summer of 1934 was the time to get your fill. Groups like the Legion of Decency were pressuring MGM, RKO, and the other studios to curb the violence and to make their movies signal loud and clear: *Crime Does Not Pay!*

A new hero was coming to the Dirty Thirties silver screen: the G-man (government man), nickname for a special agent in J. Edgar Hoover's domain, itself soon to be renamed the FBI (Federal Bureau of Investigation).

Hoover's G-men had more than a hep handle. They had new muscle. Back in the spring of 1934, Congress passed a number of laws in keeping with FDR's Twelve Point Crime Program. For one, G-men could now pack heat and make arrests. Also, racketeering, bank robbery, extortion, and taking boosted goods across state lines were among the crimes that were made federal offenses. That meant G-men could hunt for public enemies around the nation. And in July, G-men nailed Public Enemy Number One, John Dillinger. (In May, other lawmen had shot Bonnie and Clyde to death.)

The crime laws of 1934 also brought the first government gun control action: the National Firearms Act. It sought to stymie criminals' easy access to such weapons of choice as machine guns and sawed-off shotguns. The law did this by requiring registration at point of sale and laying a heavy tax on them: two hundred bucks.

Unbeknownst to the public, it was also in the spring of 1934 that FDR directed Hoover to investigate, on the q.t., profascist groups. Hoover was more than up to the task, armed as he was with the use of warrantless wiretaps and search-and-seizures.

While G-men were spying and crime-fighting to keep order, many workers were trying to catch a break by creating disorder.

Close to 1.5 million workers took part in a total of more than eighteen hundred strikes in 1934. Usually the number one demand was for management to deal in good faith with the union of the workers' choosing. Such was the case with taxi drivers in New York City, agricultural workers in California's Imperial Valley, employees of an auto parts plant in Toledo,

1933: Mexican labor activists in the cotton pickers' strike in California's San Joaquin Valley.

> " I hope you can spare the time for a few words from a cotton mill family, *out of work* and almost out of heart and in just a short while out of a house in which to live. you know of course that the realators are putting the people out when they cannot pay the rent promptly. and how are we to pay the rent so long as the mills refuse us work, merely because we had the nerve to ask or 'demand,' better working conditions. . . .
>
> hoping you'll excuse this, but I've always thought of F.D.R. as my personal friend. "

—October 1934: To FDR from a mill worker in Columbus, Georgia, and signed "C.L.F."

Place: Portland, Oregon.
Alleged crime: killing a strikebreaker.
Outcome: charges dropped.

and truckers in Minneapolis, who led the way in what became a general strike of many days.

For several days in July, California's Bay Area was in disarray when troops of workers in various fields stayed off the job in solidarity with a strike already under way: that of the San Francisco local of the ILA (International Longshoremen's Association), under the leadership of an audacious Aussie, Harry Bridges, who, like John Lewis, opposed racial discrimination in unions.

Along with union recognition, a big issue for the ILA was the shape-up. In this humiliating hiring system, dockworkers hit the piers early in the morning only to stand in a line or a semicircle *hoping* to be picked for a day's work. They were at the mercy of the hiring boss, who often gave priority to brownnosers and bribers.

The ILA strike triggered labor action beyond the Bay Area. Up and down the West Coast—from Seattle to San Diego—shipping was shut down from early May through late July.

It was in July that some twenty thousand workers in Alabama textile mills went on wildcat strikes. Soon roughly *four hundred thousand* members of the UTW (United Textile Workers) walked off the job, from the Deep South to New England. "Shorter hours! Higher wages! Reduce the working load! Recognize the union!" these people cried.

Blood flowed and chaos roamed during many strikes. Workers rioted. Police rioted. Strikers and strikebreakers brawled. Some governors called out the National Guard.

When the smoke cleared, many workers were worse off. On top of not getting spit from management, some strikers had been beaten bloody by hired goons, then fired after the strike collapsed. This was the fate of some textile workers and people who picked fruits and vegetables in the Imperial Valley.

The public had the least sympathy for this last group because most of them were Mexicans. Plus, while other unions had members who were communists and socialists, theirs was created by communists: CAWIU (Cannery and Agricultural Workers Industrial Union).

The Minneapolis teamsters were among those for whom a strike paid off. They won union recognition. So did those West Coast dockworkers. What's more, the shape-up was gone. Instead, there'd be a union-controlled hiring hall pledged to spread jobs around fairly and equally to whoever was willing to work.

While labor was on the march, FDR's critics were forming unions of their own.

Summer 1934: Harry Bridges urging his comrades to hang tough; striking textile workers in Georgia (below left); and madness in Minneapolis (below right).

September 1933: A parade on NYC's 5th Avenue in support of
the National Recovery Administration.

5

CRACKPOT IDEAS?

"For more than one hundred and fifty years the American people generally have assumed that the Federal Constitution . . . needed no continuing advocacy for its protection. Events of the past few years have indicated that this was false optimism."

This pessimism is from a fall 1934 pamphlet put out by the American Liberty League.

The league was formed in August of that year by a group of men who claimed to be motivated by love of country alone. As they saw it, the executive branch was out of control, with FDR calling too many shots (all those EOs!) and Congress rubber-stamping bills he willed, acting like a lackey. The checks and balances were out of whack, so the American Liberty League came to the rescue.

Al Smith was among its founding fathers.

> **We colored people can't organize without you and you white folks can't organize without us. Aren't we all brothers and ain't God the Father of us all? We live under the same sun . . . work on the same land, raise the same crop for the same landlord who oppresses and cheats us both. . . . The same chain that holds my people holds your people too. If we're chained together on the outside we ought to stay chained together in the union. It won't do no good for us to divide because there's where the trouble had been all the time.**

—July 1934: A founding member of STFU.

The New Deal was also under attack from former FDR boosters, now booing him for not taking more drastic action on certain fronts. Among the loudest was Louisiana senator Huey "the Kingfish" Long.

Back when Long was governor of the Pelican State, he raised taxes on corporations doing business there and turned a lot of that new revenue into schools, roads, and other good things for the general populace (which is why many in Louisiana put up with his bombast and corruption).

In early 1934, Long proposed that what he did for Louisiana should be done for the nation. "I contend, my friends, that we have no very difficult problem to solve in America," he said in a radio address. "It is not the difficulty of the problem which we have; it is the fact that the rich people of this country—and by rich people I mean the superrich—will not allow us to solve the problems, or rather the one little problem that is afflicting this country, because in order to cure all of our woes it is necessary to scale down the big fortunes, that we may scatter the wealth to be shared by all of the people."

1937: At an STFU gathering.

Problem: concentration of wealth.

Solution: redistribution of wealth.

Lest anybody *think* of calling him socialistic or Red, Long defended his plan as true-blue—practically ordained by the Declaration of Independence, which the Kingfish didn't fret about quoting correctly.

"It said, 'We hold these truths to be self-evident, that there are certain inalienable rights for the people, and among them are life, liberty, and the pursuit of happiness'; and it said, further, 'We hold the view that all men are created equal.'" Long then asked, "Now, what did they mean by that . . . that any one man was born to inherit $10 billion and that another child was to be born to inherit nothing?"

Scattering the wealth was simple, said Long.

Huey Pierce Long back in 1932 at the Democratic National Convention, where he was 110% behind FDR—and expecting favors.

Step 1: seize all personal wealth in excess of $1 million a year and supertax the superrich.

Step 2: with wealth wrenched from the rich, give each nonrich household five thousand smackeroos.

That would more than do for touchstones of the American Dream, like a house with a white picket fence and the latest Buick sedan or Chevrolet coupe.

If Long were president, his other Robin Hood moves would include a guaranteed annual income of $2,500 a year for heads of households. (At the time, the median family income was about $1,200.)

Near the end of his radio address, the Kingfish announced the birth of an outfit to ballyhoo his plan: SOW (Share Our Wealth), a society with the motto "Every man a king."

SOW societies popped up all over the nation. Long would soon claim five million followers.

SOW's motto echoed a battle cry of nineteenth-century populist William Jennings Bryan: "Every man a king, but no one wears a crown!" (Long borrowed his nickname from the fictional schemer George "Kingfish" Stevens on the hugely popular and controversial radio show *Amos 'n' Andy*.)

Millions also flocked to Father Charles Coughlin, the Radio Priest, so called because of his Sunday broadcast, *Golden Hour of the Shrine of the Little Flower*. The Shrine of the Little Flower was the name of this Roman Catholic cleric's church in Royal Oak, Michigan, about ten miles north of Detroit.

"Roosevelt or ruin!" Coughlin used to declaim.

"The New Deal is Christ's deal," he once proclaimed.

Coughlin now railed against FDR, in large part because he felt that the president hadn't bashed the Three Bs nearly enough, especially the banksters. The Radio Priest was convinced that an international cabal of that lot was behind the economic collapse.

The Radio Priest was no left-winger, but, like Huey Long, he advocated things that sounded awfully socialistic: "I believe in nationalizing those public necessities which by their very nature are too important to be held in the control of

The Radio Priest, Father Charles Edward Coughlin, who was lionized in Nazi Germany, would go down in history as a rank anti-Semite.

private individuals. By these I mean banking, credit and currency, power, light, oil and natural gas and our God-given natural resources."

While the Kingfish had his SOW, Coughlin had his NUSJ (National Union for Social Justice), launched in late 1934. By then, his *Golden Hour* aired on more than thirty stations and had about forty million listeners, many of whom formed NUSJ clubs. The radio show wouldn't be the only way for acolytes to keep up with the priest's pronouncements. Coughlin would also have a newspaper, *Social Justice*.

Circa 1935: Dr. Francis Everett Townsend.

Circa 1935: A sampling of OARP promotional material.

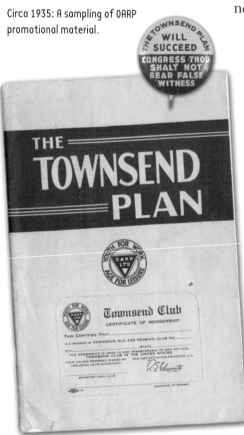

*T*ownsend's National Weekly became the bible of another grumbling group. Their leader was a retired physician, Francis Townsend, in Long Beach, California. His passion: more action on behalf of the oldsters, of which he was one—over sixty (and let go from the city's health department in 1933).

According to legend, what sparked Townsend's movement wasn't his own plight but rather a sorrowful sight in an alley near his home: three old women rummaging through trash cans for eats. The alley was a glance away from Townsend's bathroom window. He was shaving at the time.

"A torrent of invectives tore out of me," he recalled of that moment in late 1933.

When Townsend's wife, Minnie, heard him carrying on, she came running: "Oh, you mustn't shout like that. All the neighbors will hear you!"

"I want all the neighbors to hear me," he replied. "I want God Almighty to hear me! I'm going to shout until the whole country hears!"

After Townsend teamed up with Robert Clements, a real-estate agent for whom the doctor worked part-time, the country began hearing of their OARP (Old Age Revolving Pension), commonly called the Townsend Plan.

OARP advocated mandatory retirement for citizens over sixty. There were millions in that group. Legions of them had worked all their lives and would have to keep working until they keeled over. Poor seniors too feeble to work relied on charity and family. Relatively few employers had pension plans.

Under OARP, old folks wouldn't have to work themselves to death or suffer a beggar's life. Instead, they would get a government pension of $200 a month—all of which had to be spent within thirty days.

The Townsend Plan came with cure-all claims. Fewer seniors in the workforce would mean more jobs for

NEW DEAL or RAW DEAL?

Food is costing you from 50 to 150 per cent. more than it did a year ago. Here are some of the prices, THEN and NOW, in stores patronized by those who have difficulty making both ends meet.

		1933	Now	Increase
Rump or Round Roast (pound)		11c	18c	64%
Rack Lamb Chops	"	15c	25c	66%
Shoulder Lamb	"	10c	17c	70%
Pot Roast	"	10c	18c	80%
Chuck Roast	"	11c	24c	118%
Veal Chops	"	15c	32c	113%
Loin Pork	"	8½c	19c	124%
Leg of Veal	"	7½c	19c	153%
Oleomargarine	"	10½c	16½c	57%
Flour (12-pound bag)		25c	50c	100%
Bread (14 ounces)		4c	6c	50%

Above prices taken from newspaper advertisements and store circulars. And on this date (October 12, 1934) all newspapers carried the announcement of the Administration that Prices Must Go Higher.

In the higher-price stores the INCREASES have been very substantial, but in some instances are not so great as those shown above. In other words, the poorer the family, the harder it is hit.

All this is the result of the New Deal scheme for DESTROYING FOOD, in order to make it SCARCE.

A vote for Democratic candidates on November 6th is a vote to approve these increases and to send prices sky-rocketing a whole lot higher.

10   (OVER)

SO THE WORKER DOESN'T PAY TAXES!

For the State of Pennsylvania as a whole, earnings of workers are about 3 per cent. higher than they were a year ago.   *(Federal Reserve Bank, Oct. 1, 1934)*

At 1933 prices, 31 per cent. of the average worker's wages were spent for food.   *(U. S. Department of Labor)*

Food prices today are from 50 per cent. to 150 per cent. higher than they were last year.
     (Figures from representative stores)

WHAT DO THESE FACTS MEAN?

Suppose you are the head of a family and that during 1933 your earnings were $25 a week, or $1300 a year. According to the U. S. Department of Labor, you spent $400 of that $1300 for food. That left you $900 for rent, heat, light, clothing, insurance, recreation, etc.

Let's assume that you did a whole lot better than the average worker, and that your earnings now are 10 per cent. higher than they were in 1933. In that case, you are now making $1430 a year.

But the food that took $400 of your earnings during 1933, now costs you not less than $700 a year.

So, instead of having $900 left for rent, heat, light, clothing, insurance, etc., as you did last year, you have only $730 left for those other necessities now.

IN SPITE OF A 10 PER CENT. INCREASE, YOU ARE 20 PER CENT. WORSE OFF THAN YOU WERE LAST YEAR.

If you are making $25 a week now, the same as you did in 1933, then your food bill alone is taking a full one-third of what you formerly had left for other things.

THANK THE NEW DEALERS. THEY HAVE FIXED IT SO YOU CANNOT ESCAPE PAYING YOUR SHARE OF THE THOUSAND MILLION DOLLARS THEY ARE HANDING OUT FOR THE DESTRUCTION OF WHEAT, HOGS, CORN, COTTON, ETC., FOR THE SOLE PURPOSE OF MAKING FOOD SCARCE AND THEREFORE HIGH-PRICED.

                                        (OVER)

Both sides of a 1934 handbill from FDR's opposition.

everybody else. A lot of relief agencies—and expenditures—could be eliminated. Business would benefit, too, as month after month millions of seniors circulated two hundred bucks into the economy, taking care of their needs and some of their wants.

FDR filed Townsend's plan, along with Long's and Coughlin's, under "crackpot ideas." Still, the president knew these men were no laughing matter.

Hitler was a crackpot. Look how far he got.

Another Crackpot Idea?

EPIC (End Poverty in California) was the program advanced by a contender for the governorship of the Golden State in 1934: Upton Sinclair, best known for his novel *The Jungle,* on the horrors of the meatpacking industry. EPIC's central idea was for the government to confiscate idle factories and farms and turn them over to cooperatives owned and operated by unemployed industrial and agricultural workers. Sinclair didn't win, but he did get a million votes.

> There are thousands of aged women in this great and rich country who are facing poor house or suicide. . . .
>
> The suicide rate is now, one in every 27 minutes, by far there is no doubt that it will be 27 suicides in one minutes. Now there are a lot of us will choose suicide in preference to being herded into the poorhouse. . . .
>
> But if the Townsend Plan were put into effect all classes and ages would be benefitted.
>
> Therefore we ask you in the name of Humanity to use your influence for it. "

—December 1934: To ER from eighty-year-old Mrs. F.E.G. of Beverly, Massachusetts.

Circa 1930, identity unknown.

> Entering the Winter of 1934–1935, the Nation's relief load has been increasing. . . . From New York, from Chicago, where the closing of the World's Fair threw thousands out of work, from the Pennsylvania coal and steel towns, from industrial Ohio and Indiana, expecting a rise of 10 to 15 per cent by the end of February . . . from New England all the way to Texas, the story is the same. . . .
>
> In Schenectady, N.Y., there were in November 2,000 more employees on the General Electric payroll than a year ago. "But," observes an FERA investigator, "it must be remembered that in August, 1929, General Electric had 28,000 employees. Today it has 11,500. Thousands represented in that difference have been out of work so long that they have used up their savings and their credit, have exhausted the help of friends and relatives, and will have to come on relief if they don't get work soon." . . .
>
> And so they go on—the gaunt, ragged legion of the industrially damned. Bewildered, apathetic, many of them terrifyingly patient. . . .
>
> Only among the young is there evidence of revolt, apparently. "

Despite the carping from different quarters, the November 1934 midterm elections were a thumbs-up for the New Deal. The Dems increased their majority, gaining nine seats in the House and nine in the Senate—and in the process made history: never before had the party with the presidency *not* lost seats in Congress in an off-year election.

Clearly, the people had spoken, saying, *Oh, yes!* to the New Deal.

And so, while American Liberty Leaguers, the Kingfish, the Radio Priest, Dr. Townsend, and others were screaming, *Oh, no!* New Dealers were intent on thickening the alphabet soup.

The New Deal, a 1934 mural by Conrad Albrizio. Installation: the auditorium of
NYC's Leonardo da Vinci Art School at 149 E. 34th Street. Dedication: to FDR.

6

THE "SECOND NEW DEAL"

"**W**e have undertaken a new order of things." So said FDR in his January 1935 State of the Union address.

The president reported that things were looking up on the economic front and that people were looking up, too. As for him, he was looking forward to rolling on with the Four Rs— relief, recovery, reform, reconstruction.

Added to that, the watchword was security:

"1. The security of a livelihood through the better use of the national resources of the land in which we live.

2. The security against the major hazards and vicissitudes of life.

3. The security of decent homes."

The address was FDR's preface to the so-called Second New Deal.

SOME MAJOR ACTIONS DURING THE "SECOND HUNDRED DAYS"

APRIL 8 Monday

Emergency Relief Appropriation Act (what FDR calls the **"Big Bill"**) allocates close to $5 *billion* for all kinds of relief. It is the nation's biggest peacetime spending bill thus far.

MAY 1 Wednesday

By **EO,** FDR creates the **RA** (Resettlement Administration). Goal: to relocate people living on lousy farmland and in city slums to new, blue-skies communities.

MAY 6 Monday

Another **EO** births the **WPA** (Works Progress Administration). Goal: to create 3.5 million jobs (blue-collar to white-collar) and to take over FERA's direct relief duties. Harry Hopkins will head the WPA, with $1.5 billion of that Big Bill money in his till.

MAY 11 Saturday

Another **EO** results in the **REA** (Rural Electrification Administration). Goal: to improve the lives of country folks still living by the light of kerosene lamps and the sun. (Only about 11% of farms have electricity.) The REA will offer private firms and not-for-profit cooperatives low-interest loans to build power plants and string power lines.

JUNE 26 Wednesday

The **WPA,** by **EO,** gets an add-on: the **NYA** (National Youth Administration). Goal: to create jobs and job-training programs for young men *and* women ages 16 to 25.

JULY 5 Friday

National Labor Relations Act, better known as the **Wagner Act,** after New York senator Robert Wagner, who introduced the bill. It is like Section 7(a) of the NIRA, but with more might. For starters:

- Collective bargaining is a *right*.

- Collective action (like strikes) for legitimate grievances is a *right*.

- Unfair labor practices are *not all right.* Example: it is unlawful for employers to fire workers because they belong to unions, to refuse to bargain with unions, and to deal in "yellow dog" contracts (hiring people only if they vow not to join a union). However, racial and gender discrimination is not on the list of unfair practices.

AUGUST 14 Wednesday

Social Security Act leads to the **SSA** (Social Security Administration). Goal: to offer millions of Americans safety nets, including:

- Old-age pension (starting at age 65).

- Unemployment insurance.

- ADC (Aid to Dependent Children) for widows only, aka welfare.

- Grants for more social services for the blind and "for children who are crippled or who are suffering from conditions which lead to crippling."

AUGUST 23 Friday

Banking Act of 1935 makes the **FDIC** permanent. It also ups the guarantee of deposits to $5,000.

AUGUST 26 Monday

Public Utilities Holding Company Act, aka **PUHCA** (*POOH-kuh*), ushers in more regulation and oversight of holding—that is, parent—companies of gas and electric outfits. Goal: to protect consumers from being gouged. For one, holding companies are banned from owning so many utilities in one region that they amount to monopolies and thus have consumers at their mercy.

AUGUST 30 Friday

Revenue Act of 1935. Goal: to raise money by raising taxes on the wealthy.

Some say that the "Second New Deal" is a misnomer because this second wave of major action was simply a continuation of previous action and much of it was on the drawing board during the First Hundred Days.

Whatever you call the 1935 New Dealing, FDR was clearly taking the concept of a gumptious government to a new level to cure the economy and to curb social unrest.

Like the CCC, the NYA was both a helping hand and a pressure valve. There were several million young adults without income and, if high school or college dropouts, without a life plan. Crime wasn't the only concern. Groups like the Young Communist League did their best recruiting among the down-and-out and disillusioned.

Still, many conservatives saw the NYA as a waste of taxpayer dollars and yet another step down the slippery slope of the masses becoming totally dependent on the government: robbing them of their rugged individualism.

Ditto on the WPA.

This deficit spending had to stop!

But how else to deal with the still-high unemployment?

While FDR supported direct relief, he certainly didn't want it to become the American way. When he addressed Congress back in January 1935, he stressed, "We must and shall quit this business of relief." He likened the dole to a drug: "a subtle destroyer of the human spirit."

The difference between FDR and his critics on the Right was his belief that if the government was going to move people *off* relief, it had to move them *to* something. Something salutary to the human spirit. And so, the start and continuation of agencies such as the WPA and the CCC.

FDR looked forward to the government quitting the business of work relief, too. That's why, say, construction workers on a WPA-built courthouse would earn more than they would receive were they on the dole, but less than what would be a fair wage for the same work in the private sector. Like the

> **"I'm sick I hate life. I go with my friends to school sometimes But they don't appreciate me because I'm poor and haven't got clothes like they do. . . . I hate every thing now because life seems blind I love my mother dearly my dad works 3 dys a wk he gets $40 a mth. But he has lot of old bills to pay from before when he did not work I wish I had work I would help my dad although he is mean to me."**
>
> —Early 1934: To ER from a fifteen-year-old girl, M.S., in Clairton, Pennsylvania.

dole, work relief was there to keep the wolf from the door until a person found a better-paying job in the private sector. Still, FDR caught flak.

Also under attack, the Revenue Act. FDR had called it a "wealth tax" back when he pitched it to the Senate, asking for a big hike in taxes on incomes and inheritances of the super-rich, as well as on corporate profits, among other things.

Huey Long began acting the fool on the Senate floor as the president's message was read aloud.

"Amen!" said the Kingfish of the bill.

The moneybags who branded FDR a traitor to his class called it a "soak the rich" bill. They were still doing that after the Revenue Act was a done deal, but that was just posturing.

The final bill wasn't all that fierce. Most in Congress didn't itch to soak the rich. The fact that the Revenue Act raised the tax rate on individual incomes of $5 million and over to 79 percent sounded like a big deal, but it wasn't. Oil tycoon John D. Rockefeller was the only person to whom that applied. (The tax on individual incomes of $1 million to $5 million remained at 63 percent.)

FDR was fine with the watered-down bill. He had been posturing, too. What he cared about was *appearing* to want to soak the rich and "stealing Huey Long's thunder," as he told brain truster Ray Moley.

Of all the commandos of crackpot ideas, Long was the one who gave FDR a worry. Everyone knew that Long had the lust and the guts to run for president. (Townsend had no presidential aspirations, and even if the Radio Priest had wanted to run, he couldn't have because he was born in Canada.)

> **❝ Huey Long is the man we thought you were when we voted for you.❞**
>
> —1935: To FDR from W. E. Warren, head of a small bank in Montana.

Labor, of course, hip-hip-hoorayed over the Wagner Act. Within a few months of its passage, there was a new organization within the AFL: the CIO (Committee for Industrial Organization). Spearheaded and presided over by John Lewis, the CIO strove to increase the number of industrial unions.

Not surprisingly, big business fumed over the Wagner Act, as it did over PUHCA, which could have been dubbed the No-More-Sam-Insull-Type-Antics Act.

British-born, Chicago-based Sam Insull had not exactly started out in rags, but he ended up with riches, rising from Thomas Edison's private secretary to a mighty merchant of power, with a vast network of utility companies in a tangled web of holding companies that operated in more than thirty states. Along the way, as Insull eliminated the competition, he raised customers' rates. He also got into investment banking, doing brisk business selling stock in his companies.

September 1935: Labor Day parade on San Francisco's Market Street.

Sam Insull had once been praised for his business acumen, but by 1931 people wanted to stone him. He had been cooking the books. On paper, his holdings seemed to be in great financial shape. In reality, his empire was $20 million in debt. When his house of cards collapsed in the wake of the crash, several hundred thousand investors lost their shirts.

Insull hotfooted it out of the country after he was indicted for fraud, embezzlement, and other crimes in 1932. His search for a safe haven was in vain. Turkey turned in seventy-three-year-old Insull and sent him back to the States, where he faced trial—which, to the dismay of many, ended in acquittal.

Not only did New Dealers have Insull in mind when they came up with PUHCA, but was also one of the poster boys for the need for the 1933 Truth in Securities Act and the creation of the SEC in 1934.

The Social Security Act, regarded as the New Deal's biggest deal, especially had conservatives crying, *Socialism!* while genuine socialists sucked their teeth. Chief beef: the people eligible for an old-age pension would partially fund it through a payroll tax starting at 1 percent and set to rise to 3 percent in a few years, no matter how much a person earned. So it was a regressive tax: taking a bigger bite out of the paychecks of low-wage workers. (A person making $100 a month will miss $3 more than a person making $1,000 will miss $30.) Not surprising, many employers weren't thrilled that they, too, had to pony up for pensions. (And the same held for unemployment insurance.)

There were members of FDR's administration who had balked at the payroll tax—some on pure humanitarian grounds, others out of concern for the economy. The more money that came out of people's paychecks, the less they'd have to consume—and consumption was vital to keep shops open and farms and factories humming.

FDR had been adamant about the taxes. Better a pinch now than a poke later.

"We put those payroll contributions there so as to give the contributors a legal, moral, and political right to collect their pensions and the unemployment benefits," he would one day say. "With those taxes in there, no damn politician can ever scrap my social security program."

The Left was also upset with the president's program because so many people were still out in the cold: millions of agricultural and domestic workers, a significant number of whom were blacks and other people of color.

FDR had once dreamed of an all-encompassing social security scheme. "There is no reason why everybody in the United States should not be covered," he had said to Frances

August 14, 1935: FDR signing the Social Security Act, surrounded by ardent supporters of the bill. In a dark suit and standing almost shoulder to shoulder with Frances Perkins is Senator Robert Wagner. Remarked FDR in his signing statement: "If the Senate and the House of Representatives in this long and arduous session had done nothing more than pass this Bill, the session would be regarded as historic for all time."

Let's Leave Out the Joker

SOCIALISTIC

EXPERIMENTS

ROOSEVELT "NEW DEAL"

From the April 17, 1933, *Boston Transcript.*

Perkins when the social security program was on the drawing board. "I see no reason why every child, from the day he is born, shouldn't be a member of the social security system. When he begins to grow up, he should know he will have old-age benefits direct from the insurance system to which he will belong all his life. If he is out of work, he gets a benefit. If he is sick or crippled, he gets a benefit."

As FDR saw it, no one should be left out in the cold: "And there is no reason why just the industrial workers should get the benefit of this. Everybody ought to be in on it. . . . I don't see why not. . . . Cradle to the grave . . . they ought to be in a social security insurance system."

FDR later realized that his great dream was not possible. For one, too much social insurance would have sparked even louder cries of *Socialism!*

While the president did the dreaming, Frances Perkins did the work. FDR had put her in charge of the committee that hammered out the who, what, when, where, and how. She then drafted the final bill, which Senator Wagner introduced in the Senate.

(As for Townsendites, they were disappointed in the government's pension plan. It fell far short of the two hundred bucks they called for. On average, monthly Social Security checks would range from about $10 to $85.)

Around the start of the Second Hundred Days, American Liberty Leaguers and like-minded folks had something to cheer. The Blue Eagle had been zapped by the case of the "sick chickens," as *A.L.A. Schechter Poultry Corp. v. United States* is known.

The NRA had charged Schechter Poultry, in Brooklyn, New York, with several violations. They included not adhering to codes for wages and hours and selling bad chickens. The case ended up before the Supreme Court, with the defense contending that the NRA was unconstitutional. The Court agreed.

The justices did not sanction the way the poultry company did business, but they found that the part of the act that created the NRA had overreached. It had, in essence, given the federal government a say over *intra*state commerce when, according to the Constitution, Uncle Sam could only have a say on *inter*state matters. The decision, handed down in May 1935, was unanimous.

When the NRA was abolished, so was Section 7(a). The New Dealers' comeback for that: the Wagner Act.

The NRA wasn't the only New Deal action SCOTUS squashed. Most notably, the AAA was invalidated in January 1936. The Court ruled that the processing tax was unconstitutional because the government was essentially making one party (say, a miller) pay another party (a farmer).

It was a 6–3 decision. Two justices not wholly hostile to the New Deal had agreed with the Court's four archconservatives: James Clark McReynolds, George Sutherland, Willis Van Devanter, and Pierce Butler. New Dealers dubbed these justices the Battalion of Death.

While contending with the Battalion of Death's apparent animus, New Dealers continued to get cheers from everyday people—for starters, the millions once broke and hungry who now had jobs with the PWA, WPA, and other alphabet soup agencies. Hundreds of thousands more—from agency chiefs to clerical workers and cleaners—were cogs in the ever-growing government bureaucracy. Plus, those 1933 cuts in salaries of government employees and vets' benefits had been rescinded (in 1934 and 1935). Even many people still getting a raw deal kept their faith in FDR.

_____

Countering the End of the Triple A

February 1936
An amendment to the 1935 **Soil Conservation and Domestic Allotment Act** seeks to control agricultural production in the guise of an environmental measure and matter of national food security. Farmers will be paid to grow soybeans and other soil-nourishing plants in place of soil-robbing crops such as cotton and corn.

> **Dear Mr. President,**
> **Would you please direct the people in charge of the releaf work in Georgia to issue the provisions + other supplies to our suffering colored people. I am sorry to worrie you with this Mr. President but hard as it is to believe the releaf officials here are using up most every thing that you send for them self + their friends. they give out the releaf supplies here on Wednesday of this week and give us black folks, each one, nothing but a few cans of pickle meet and to white folks they give blankets, bolts of cloth and things like that. . . . Please help us mr President. . . . Yours truly cant sign my name Mr President they will beat me up and run me away from here.**

—October 1935: From Reidsville, Georgia.

People with a heart for the arts—especially artists—were ecstatic about the WPA's public arts project. When Harry Hopkins launched it in the summer of 1935, Uncle Sam was set to become the nation's biggest patron of the arts. (To people who balked at the idea of artists on the government payroll, Hopkins's standing response was "Hell, they've got to eat just like other people." His FERA had included an arts project.)

And so, the WPA's FMP (Federal Music Project) will give concerts in symphony halls, as well as in amphitheaters, hospitals, schools, prisons, and CCC camps. There'll be Mozart and Mendelssohn. There'll be jazz. There'll be tributes to cowboy culture by the likes of the Arbuckle Buckaroos, along with Serbo-Croatian, Appalachian, and Hungarian bands, too.

For some of its promotional materials, the FMP will turn to the FAP (Federal Art Project).

Through the FAP, visual artists will make a cornucopia of art—from murals to sculptures—for parks, post offices, and other public spaces. Some artists will teach free art classes in schools and at FAP-sponsored community art centers. Along

A Few New Deal Stats (1933–1935)

- National income was up by more than 50%.
- Unemployment was down from over 12 million in March 1933 to 8 million—with about 70% of the unemployed getting some relief through a stint with the WPA.
- Farm income was up, to nearly $7 billion (versus roughly $2 billion in late 1932).
- Since its inception in June 1933, HOLC had helped roughly 4 million families hang on to their homes.

with making promotional material for the FMP and for its own exhibits, the FAP will produce posters to raise awareness of all kinds of things, from the joys of local zoos to the importance of water conservation and the benefits of drinking milk.

Another piece of FAP work: posters for productions of the FTP (Federal Theatre Project).

The FTP will employ thousands of actors, directors, set designers, costume designers, stagehands, and other talents it takes to put on shows, from marionette plays to musical revues.

The cutting-edge Living Newspaper unit will offer ripped-from-the-headlines dramatizations of social issues. FTP's daring adaptations of classics will include a black-cast *Macbeth* set in Haiti, directed by the up-and-coming iconoclastic Orson Welles (several years away from scaring the bejeebers out of people with his radio broadcast *The War of the Worlds* and awing moviegoers with *Citizen Kane,* based on the lives of several tycoons, including Sam Insull and William Randolph Hearst).

The FTP will also mount works by contemporary writers, including Sinclair Lewis, producing an adaptation of his satirical novel *It Can't Happen Here,* about an apple-pie American becoming a fascist dictator. He's a man who embraces crackpot ideas, including some of Huey Long's.

Some FTP plays will be penned by people working for the FWP (Federal Writers' Project).

While some FWP hires write plays, others will collect and catalog Americana, from historical records and folklore to oral history projects, such as the one devoted to black remembrances of slavery. The FWP's signature work will be the American Guide Series: tours of states, cities, regions, and territories. (Down the road, FWP workers will answer the call to submit some off-the-clock work to *American Stuff: An Anthology of Prose and Verse,* issued by a commercial publisher.)

" All of this music belongs to the nation. "

—FMP's first national director, Nikolai Sokoloff, the Cleveland Orchestra's former conductor.

Thank You, Uncle Sam!

The list of performing, literary, and fine artists who were grateful for a WPA paycheck includes:

Conrad Aiken	Burt Lancaster
Nelson Algren	Jacob Lawrence
Nathan Asch	Canada Lee
Saul Bellow	Rosetta LeNoire
Arna Bontemps	José Limón
John Cheever	Sidney Lumet
Joseph Cotten	E. G. Marshall
Willem de Kooning	Jackson Pollock
Katherine Dunham	John Randolph
Ralph Ellison	Augusta Savage
Arlene Francis	Studs Terkel
Will Geer	Margaret Walker
John Houseman	Orson Welles
Zora Neale Hurston	Eudora Welty
Ezra Jack Keats	Richard Wright
Arthur Kennedy	

" Theatre, when it's good, is always dangerous. "

—FTP's first and only national director, Hallie Flanagan, founder of Vassar College's Experimental Theatre. When she was a student at Iowa's Grinnell College, Harry Hopkins was among her classmates.

" I might not have been [an actor]. I might not have made it if it hadn't been for the Federal Theatre. "

—E. G. Marshall. His long television and movie career included playing Juror 4 in *Twelve Angry Men*, a fictional president in *Superman II*, a real president in *Ike*, and Dr. Thurmond on *Chicago Hope*.

> **There is plenty of first-rate talent among our writers and this talent demands an outlet.**
>
> —FWP's first national director, Henry Alsberg, former lawyer, journalist, theater director, and editor of two FERA publications.

> **Art should belong to the people as a whole.**
>
> —FAP's first and only national director, Holger Cahill, art critic, curator, and former acting director of New York City's MoMA.

Clockwise from top left across spread: A poster by an artist working for the FAP in Illinois (1936); scene from *The Emperor's New Clothes,* mounted by the FTP's children's unit in NYC (1935); scene from the FTP Living Newspaper *Triple-A Plowed Under* (1936, in NYC), in which the actor playing Al Smith (the tall one) hurrahs the demise of the AAA; another FAP poster; scene from *Young Tramps,* put on by the FTP's dance unit (1935, in NYC).

Shirley Temple likes milk

Smile and be Happy

CURE JUVENILE DELINQUENCY IN THE SLUMS BY PLANNED HOUSING

NEW YORK CITY
HOUSING AUTHORITY

Clockwise from top left across spread: FAP poster on housing in NYC (October 1936); FDR with a relief recipient in Bismarck, North Dakota (August 1936); beneficiaries of the WPA's school lunch program (1936, place unknown); a WPA worker in Detroit with his first paycheck (October 1935); a 1936 article on an RA town in Maryland (May 1936); NYA library assistants in Illinois (circa 1936, city unknown); NYA office workers, also in Illinois (circa 1936); WPA chief Harry Hopkins in Seattle (September 1936); PWA-sponsored work-in-progress on the Pacific Northwest's Bonneville Dam (October 1936); future U.S. president LBJ, center, on the job as an NYA administrator at a roadside park in Seguin, Texas (early 1936).

MORE ALPHABET SOUP ACTION

> " You know a hungry man is dangerous but a hungry man with a family is twice dangerous to any community. I don't know whether other people ever thought of it or not but, to me, WPA employment certainly has had its moral effect upon the people and to my way of thinking has kept many a good man from turning thief or bank robber. "

—From an interview with a twenty-eight-year-old man in Kentucky

Greenbelt, the New Deal's Model Suburb

Lobby card for the 1936 hit flick about a country bumpkin, Longfellow Deeds, who inherits $20 million after the death of an uncle (a banker). Instead of longing for ritzy cars and caviar, Longfellow wants to share the wealth.

7
RENDEZVOUS WITH DESTINY

In June 1936, a *Fortune* magazine poll revealed that 53 percent of the nation reckoned that FDR had kicked out Depression.

That was far from true. Millions were still unemployed. Perception, however, is often everything. The fact that so many people *felt* that hard times were over was a big smile back at FDR, already confident that he would have a second term and feeling measurably less embattled.

"I am fighting Communism, Huey Longism, Coughlinism, Townsendism," he had told a reporter in 1935, "to save our system, the capitalist system."

With the "Second New Deal," FDR had stolen *a lot* of people's thunder. As for Huey Long, he was absolutely, positively no longer a threat.

The Kingfish was dead.

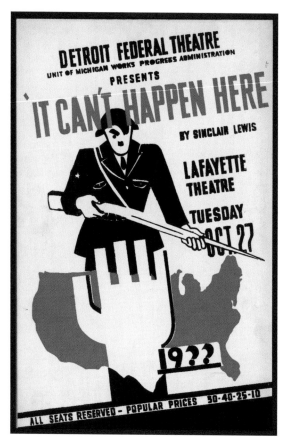

Lewis's play about fascism coming to America premiered in October 1936 in ten cities.

Back on September 8, 1935, in Baton Rouge, Huey Long was shot while exiting the statehouse. His bodyguards quickly tackled the man closest at hand and shot him more than fifty times. He was Dr. Carl Weiss, son-in-law of a Louisiana judge on whom Long had played some political dirty tricks.

When the Kingfish passed on September 10 (not of his wounds but of a medical blunder), his followers were devastated: in August he had thrown his hat into the ring to be the Dems' next presidential candidate.

SOW basically died with its founder.

Shucks! So thought Long's right-hand man, Gerald Smith, a former Disciples of Christ minister enamored with the Silver Shirts, an American pro-Nazi group.

Having tried and failed miserably to become SOW's new king and determined at least to co-lead *something,* Smith joined forces with Dr. Townsend and the Radio Priest.

Result: the Union Party.

Its presidential candidate: North Dakota representative William Lemke.

Its thrust: FDR is the Antichrist. (Lemke was livid with FDR for not supporting a 1936 bill that would have expanded the New Deal for farmers.)

The GOP fielded the oilman Alf Landon, governor of the Sunflower State. Landon's folksy ways and compassionate conservative persona gave a host of Republicans hope that the Kansan would draw many Dems into the GOP tent.

From the Campaign Trail, 1936

WELCOME FATHER COUGHLIN HEAD OF N.U.S.J.

INDEPENDENT COALITION AM... WO...

STRIKE OUT the NEW DEAL

The Independent Coalition of American Women was an American Liberty League auxiliary.

UNION PARTY LEMKE O'BRIEN

Lemke is on the left. His running mate, Tom O'Brien, was a lawyer from Massachusetts.

July 1936: The Radio Priest tipping into FDR at OARP's national convention in Cleveland, where Townsendites officially endorsed the Union Party.

Landon's running mate, Frank Knox, was the publisher of the *Chicago Daily News*.

Earl Browder, an accountant from Kansas, succeeded William Foster as the CPUSA's chief. Ford is the same James Ford who was the party's VP pick in 1932.

FOR A FREE, HAPPY, PROSPEROUS AMERICA BROWDER FOR PRESIDENT FORD FOR VICE PRES VOTE COMMUNIST

DEMOCRAT FOR LANDON

LANDON DEEDS NOT DEFICITS

VOTE FOR THOMAS NELSON SOCIALISM

Norman Thomas's running mate, George Nelson, was a Wisconsin farmer.

THE RUBBER STAMP

THIS SPACE FOR MESSAGE

Why stand for this sort of thing longer? Elect Republicans to Congress and return the country to real representative government.

YES SIR! YES SIR! ANYTHING ELSE SIR? DIG IN NEW DEAL PORK BARREL BLANK CHECKS BILLS NEW DEAL CONGRESS RRA GUFFEY AAA

In this anti-FDR postcard, the "Guffey" bill in the wastebasket refers to a law regulating the soft-coal industry on which SCOTUS put the kibosh in 1936.

PROMISE AND PERFORMANCE

The Administration of FRANKLIN D. ROOSEVELT REVEALS ITSELF

This pamphlet from the Republican National Committee counts the ways that FDR let down the nation, in its opinion.

Logo.

This pro-CPUSA pamphlet casts the American Liberty League as a maniacal menace, seeking a dictatorship of big business. Flanking Al Smith are Irénée (left) and Pierre du Pont. Ironically, in 1937 FDR Jr. will marry Ethel du Pont, whose father, Eugene, was an American Liberty League founding member.

Lemke, Landon, and all the other contenders—gnats to a giant. That's how FDR felt. He had no fear.

"We have conquered fear," he declared in his acceptance speech during the Democratic National Convention in late June 1936 at Philly's Franklin Field. "This is fitting ground on which to reaffirm the faith of our fathers; to pledge ourselves to restore to the people a wider freedom; to give to 1936 as the founders gave to 1776—an American way of life."

His speech was a praise song to liberty.

"Liberty requires opportunity to make a living—a living decent according to the standard of the time, a living which gives man not only enough to live by, but something to live for."

FDR lashed out at the "economic royalists" who "have maintained that economic slavery was nobody's business" and who "complain that we seek to overthrow the institutions of America. What they really complain of is that we seek to take away their power. . . . In vain they seek to hide behind the Flag

January 1936: Some of the 2,000 attendees of the American Liberty League's banquet at D.C.'s Mayflower Hotel. There, Al Smith lambasted FDR and the New Deal as un-American and intimated that if FDR won the nomination, he himself would quit the Democratic Party.

THE WINNER
(PAGE 7)

NEWS-WEEK
The Illustrated News-Magazine
Vol. VIII, No. 19   NOVEMBER 7, 1936   Ten Cents

Cactus Jack was FDR's
running mate again.

and the Constitution. In their blindness they forget what the Flag and the Constitution stand for. Now, as always, they stand for democracy, not tyranny; for freedom, not subjection; and against a dictatorship by mob rule and the over-privileged alike."

At the end of this speech, FDR spoke of "a mysterious cycle in human events." Paraphrasing a passage from the New Testament's Gospel of Luke, he said that to some generations "much is given," while of others "much is expected." Then came the most entrancing, if enigmatic, line: "This generation of Americans has a rendezvous with destiny."

And he, with a second term.

This time around, the nation didn't have to wait four months for the president to be sworn in. The Twentieth Amendment to the Constitution (ratified back in 1933) changed the month of Inauguration Day and the new Congress's convening to January, effective 1937.

The weather was worse on January 20, 1937, than on Inauguration Day 1933. The nation's capital was under a deluge.

With no umbrella over his hatless head and his rain-splotched speech before him, FDR was again majestic. Most memorable was his plaint for the poor:

I see millions of families trying to live on incomes so meager that the pall of family disaster hangs over them day by day.

I see millions whose daily lives in city and on farm continue under conditions labeled indecent by a so-called polite society half a century ago.

I see millions denied education, recreation, and the opportunity to better their lot and the lot of their children.

I see millions lacking the means to buy the products of farm and factory and by their poverty denying work and productiveness to many other millions.

I see one-third of a nation ill-housed, ill-clad, ill-nourished.

Summer 1936: A sharecropper's cabin in Hale County, Alabama, photographed by RA staffer Walker Evans. He and writer James Agee were in rural Alabama doing an article on sharecroppers for *Fortune* magazine, which killed the story in the end. Walker and Agee's work became their classic exploration of rural poverty, *Let Us Now Praise Famous Men* (1941).

FDR was not in a state of despair, but rather painting this picture "in hope—because the Nation, seeing and understanding the injustice in it, proposes to paint it out. We are determined to make every American citizen the subject of his country's interest and concern."

As he spoke, labor had capital very concerned.

Labor—especially the CIO—had gotten out the vote big-time for FDR, and John Lewis's UMW alone contributed half a million bucks to FDR's campaign coffers. The president hadn't made any promises, but labor expected attention to be paid.

And by 1936, labor was more of a lion. Lewis had done a bang-up job unionizing more industrial workers. The UAW (United Automobile Workers) and SWOC (Steel Workers Organizing Committee) were two of his new CIO unions.

"We must capitalize on the election," said Lewis in the wake of FDR's landslide—not that the rank and file needed to be told that.

Starting in late 1936 and continuing into 1937, there were more than four thousand strikes. Most were the walkout kind. Others were the sit-down type—workers took over the joint.

That's what happened to giant GM, with some sixty plants in more than a dozen states, and producing about 50 percent of the nation's cars (along with pickup trucks and other vehicles). The company's 1936 *net* profit: roughly $240 million.

Like at other companies, one way GM increased profits was through the speedup: making assembly line workers move at a sickeningly fast pace. Until they said *Enough!*

GM was hit with sit-down strikes in several cities, including Atlanta, Cleveland, Kansas City, and—the big hit—Flint, home to several GM factories. Flint's Fisher Body Plant 1—

"Roosevelt is the first president of the century who has given more than lip service to labor. He hasn't gone as far as we'd like. But he's learning. If he keeps on learning—all right! If he doesn't—"

—An unidentified CIO official in the December 5, 1936, *Liberty* magazine.

Barely readable at the bottom of this circa 1936 UMW pin is the year of the union's founding: 1890.

Early 1937: Flint, Michigan. The sit-down strikes there started on December 30, 1936. This was two days after the sit-down at a Cleveland plant that made the bodies for GM's Chevys.

the biggest auto body plant on the planet—had the only set of body dies for most of GM's 1937 American brands (Pontiacs and Cadillacs, among them).

The war on GM lasted for days, then weeks. Management was furious that neither Michigan's governor, the recently elected pro-labor Frank Murphy, nor FDR dispatched troops to oust the strikers. They *were* trespassing on private property, after all. FDR and Governor Murphy, however, feared that if soldiers stormed the plants, the Wolverine State might erupt in a civil war.

"Is that you, Bill?"

This was FDR on the telephone with GM's current president, William Knudsen, in early February 1937. FDR had placed the call at Frances Perkins's urging. She believed a little presidential persuasion might end the deadlock.

And so FDR told Knudsen that he was unhappy about what both management and the workers were going through. (GM shareholders were none too pleased, either. GM had averaged two thousand cars a day. Now that number had dropped to about twenty. Fewer cars. Lower sales. Less profit.)

GM soon capitulated. The company was ready to meet with Lewis and forge a new deal with autoworkers that would start with recognition of the UAW. (By then, its membership was about 166,000, up from 88,000 in December 1936.)

March 1937: In NYC.

After what happened to GM, some corporations decided to deal with unions, figuring that it was only a matter of time before they got hit with a walkout or a sit-down strike. U.S. Steel was a prime target. This, the nation's biggest steel producer, had long been acutely anti-union.

So jaws dropped when, in early March 1937, U.S. Steel announced that it was ready to recognize the CIO's SWOC. The outcome included an eight-hour day, a forty-hour week, and a minimum wage of five dollars a day with time and a half for overtime.

Ford, Westinghouse, and Republic Steel were among the scores of corporations that didn't follow U.S. Steel's lead. Result: more strikes—and more bloodstained days—some coming in May, the month of the original Labor Day.

May 26, 1937: Dearborn, Michigan, outside Ford's River Rouge plant during the Battle of the Overpass, so called because it was on the Miller Road overpass that Ford "servicemen" and freelance thugs attacked UAW organizers. The man being beaten is UAW official Dick Frankensteen. Also injured that day: the union's future legendary president, Walter Reuther (thrown down the overpass steps after a throttling).

May 28, 1937: Struthers, Ohio. A show of solidarity with workers on strike against the steel manufacturer Youngstown Sheet & Tube.

Everybody's nerves were frayed.

Early on, strikers had a lot of sympathy from around the nation. Now labor seemed scary—too militant, too radical, fostering too much chaos. It was no secret that many workers who had once belonged to CPUSA unions had joined AFL unions, especially those in the CIO wing. Communists hoped to instigate revolution from within.

As for FDR, he was disgusted with both labor and capital, feeling, *A plague on both your houses!*

On top of all this, he was still smoldering over his war on the Battalion of Death.

The SCOTUS in place when FDR became POTUS in 1932. *Standing, left to right:* Owen Josephus Roberts, Pierce Butler, Harlan Fiske Stone, and Benjamin Nathan Cardozo. *Seated, left to right:* Louis Dembitz Brandeis, Willis Van Devanter, Charles Evans Hughes (chief justice), James Clark McReynolds, and George Sutherland.

ROOSEVELT *AND* RUIN?

"Justice McReynolds will still be on the bench when he is a hundred and five years old."

This was FDR's response to a politician's suggestion that the president simply bide his time instead of scheming to nudge out or neutralize McReynolds and the other conservative Supreme Court justices.

McReynolds and the rest of the Battalion of Death—Butler, Van Devanter, Sutherland—were seventy or older (as were two other justices).

FDR didn't want to wait until they decided to retire or died. He wanted more judges who were liberal as soon as possible.

Given the fate of the NRA and the AAA, FDR feared that SCOTUS would undo more of the New Deal. And the president certainly had reason to fear this.

This quadruple C stood for the Citizens Committee for Court and Constitution, a group that rose up in protest against FDR's court-packing plan.

> " A liberal cause was never won by stacking a deck of cards, by stuffing a ballot box, or by packing a court. "
>
> —1937: Senator Burton Wheeler (D-MT).

Legal challenges to the constitutionality of some "Second New Deal" actions were in the works, with the American Liberty League funding some of these lawsuits. On the hit list: the Social Security Act, the Wagner Act, and PUHCA.

Thus, in February 1937, the president leaned on Congress to pass a bill that would let him increase the number of federal and Supreme Court justices. For every judge who did not retire at age seventy, he could appoint an additional one (with a maximum of forty-four for federal courts and six for SCOTUS).

To garner support for what FDR called court reform and others called court packing, the president tried to charm the press and members of Congress. He even had a fireside chat. His spin: that he was looking out for the justices, trying to lighten the seniors' workload.

Didn't work. People of all political persuasions were appalled. Even Cactus Jack bailed on FDR.

Interestingly, by the time FDR's court bill was defeated in July 1937, SCOTUS had ruled on the Social Security Act, the Wagner Act, and PUHCA. Not a one was deemed unconstitutional. All were left intact. What's more, the conservative justice Van Devanter had announced his retirement.

The man FDR chose to replace him drew squawks from different quarters: Alabama senator Hugo Black, ex–KKK member turned liberal.

Many white Southerners had opposed FDR's court-packing scheme out of fear that more liberal judges would benefit blacks. Almost since its inception in 1909, one way the NAACP sought Jim Crow's overthrow was through lawsuits. The New Deal inspired more of that. It also had black America at large looking to FDR's administration for a better deal.

Since the nineteenth century, most blacks who could vote had cast their ballots for GOP candidates. The Republican

Party was the party of Emancipation and of other liberating laws during Reconstruction, most notably the Fourteenth Amendment (citizenship) and the Fifteenth Amendment (voting rights for men). Even after Reconstruction and the actual and figurative death of Radical Republicans, most blacks remained loyal to the GOP. Then, in the election of 1936, the majority went for FDR, making up one component of the New Deal coalition (with farmers and industrial workers among the others).

Though blacks weren't getting an equal deal, they were at least getting some alphabet soup (jobs with the WPA and the CCC, for example). They also had allies and well-wishers in FDR's administration.

February 1, 1937: Louisville, Kentucky. This ironic and iconic photo of happy-go-lucky characters in a billboard looming above real people on a relief line in the wake of the great Ohio River flood was taken by Margaret Bourke-White on assignment for *Life* magazine.

Take Secretary of the Interior Harold Ickes. He pressed contractors on PWA projects to hire black skilled workers. He also mandated the slating of a substantial amount of low-income housing for blacks.

Like white tenants in PWA housing, blacks benefited from Ickes's vision of low-income housing: solidly built, for starters, and outfitted with things many people didn't think those at the bottom of the economic pyramid deserved. Things like closets with doors. (A good deal of PWA housing had electric stoves and refrigerators, which 80 percent of American households didn't have.)

While segregation remained in effect, Ickes kicked out some Jim Crow in his domain, desegregating the Department of the Interior's public facilities (the cafeteria, for example). Ickes also gave blacks jobs in his department. His most notable black hire was economist Robert Weaver, assistant adviser on black affairs.

And then there was the First Lady.

ER's travels around the country had opened her eyes to the plight of black folks. So had reports from Lorena Hickok. ER had also gotten to know Mary McLeod Bethune, president of Bethune-Cookman College in Florida and head of the largest black women's civic organization, the NCNW (National Council of Negro Women).

Fall 1935: Harold Ickes signing a document pertaining to self-rule on a reservation in Montana, stemming from the controversial Wheeler-Howard Act of 1934, aka the IRA (Indian Reorganization Act), aka the Indian New Deal, aka the Back-to-the-Blanket Plan. Behind him stand Salish and Kootenai tribal leaders and John Collier, Commissioner of Indian Affairs.

ER had tapped Bethune to serve on the NYA's advisory board. FDR topped that by making Bethune the first black woman to head a department in the federal government when he appointed her director of a new NYA department: the Division of Negro Affairs. And she was not FDR's only black appointee. But he was not about to go on a civil rights crusade.

It was to keep the white South from revolting that FDR refused to support an antilynching bill that sought to deter lynching by making it a federal crime. Lynching, more prevalent in the South, was largely used to terrorize blacks.

FDR had no love for lynchers; he thought them despicable. Still—

No can do. That was his final answer to NAACP chief Walter White on backing the antilynching bill. "I did not choose the tools with which I must work," said the president. "Had I been permitted to choose them I would have selected quite different ones. But I've got to get legislation passed by Congress to save America." He noted that Southerners chaired or occupied "strategic places on most of the Senate and House

March 1938: Front and center is Mary McLeod Bethune, surrounded by members of an action/advisory committee she organized, composed of other blacks with posts of note. This "Black Cabinet" had no official power, but they did have FDR's ear. In the 1960s, Robert Weaver (front row, third from left) would become the first black person to hold a real cabinet position (Secretary of HUD).

1937 Add-ins to the Alphabet Soup
by Acts of Congress

July 22
The **FSA** (Farm Security Administration) to combat rural poverty largely by setting up cooperative communities for tenant farmers and other agricultural workers whom landowners or Mother Nature had displaced. The FSA replaces Rex Tugwell's Resettlement Administration.

November 1
The **USHA** (United States Housing Authority) to help the ill-housed, chiefly by lending local housing authorities money at very favorable terms to build public housing (and in the process take over the PWA's housing division). USHA's initial loan fund: $500 million. Lending cap: 90% of a project's cost.

committees. If I come out for the anti-lynching bill now, they will block every bill I ask Congress to pass to keep America from collapsing. I just can't take that risk."

By late 1937, the president was at risk of being condemned a failure. The U.S. economy hit stormy weather: the "Roosevelt Recession."

Just when happy days seemed to be here again, FDR decided, quite inexplicably, that a balanced budget was the order of the day. Result: spending cuts. The fallout included the loss of 140,000 PWA and 500,000 WPA jobs. This came at a time when some economists were urging the president to stop worrying about deficits and to spend even more.

With FDR's reverse action, consumption began to slump. Rising unemployment wasn't the only cause. Those Social Security payroll taxes had started to kick in. As millions of people began tightening their belts, businesses started doing the same thing. Then, in October 1937, the stock market began to tumble.

Oh, Lord. People began to panic.

And FDR was furious.

The president was convinced that the downturn was the work of the "economic royalists"—fat cats sitting on gobs of cash, but holding back from investing in the stock market as well as in business expansion and start-ups. That's how big business goes on strike.

Manhattan's original Rockefeller Center, a twelve-acre, fourteen-building complex in the making, was an example of what deep pockets could do. Groundbreaking on this art deco marvel had occurred two years after the crash, in 1931 (and the project would generate about seventy-five thousand jobs).

Some would argue that those who did not do as Rockefeller had were motivated by caution, not spite.

Harold Ickes was among the New Dealers who disagreed. He made that clear in a December 1937 radio address, "It Is Happening Here."

"To the 120,000,000 people of the United States, [wealthy business owners] have made the threat," fumed Ickes, "that unless they are free to speculate free of regulations . . . unless they are free to accumulate through legal tricks . . . unless they are free to dominate the rest of us . . . unless they are once more free to do all these things, then the United States is to have its first general sit-down strike—not of labor—not of the American people—of the sixty families."

The "sixty families" was code for the superrich popularized by Ferdinand Lundberg's controversial book *America's Sixty Families* (1937). It charged that a very tiny minority of Americans who ruled big business controlled the nation, from the press to politics.

Don't be bullied! Ickes urged. "If the American people yield to this bluff [of the sixty families], then the America that is to be will be a big-business Fascist America—an enslaved America."

While people debated whether big business had gone on strike, FDR reverted to deficit spending. Funding for the alphabet soup went up. But not Roosevelt's clout.

In the 1938 midterm elections, history did not repeat. Whereas in 1934 the Dems had picked up nine seats in both houses of Congress, in November 1938 they lost six seats in the Senate and more than ten times that number in the House. What's more, a bunch of anti–New Deal Democrats had beat out pro–New Deal Democrats, most notably in the South. This despite the vigorous stumping FDR had done for the latter (his attempted party "purge").

1938 New Deals

February 10

An amendment to the law that created the FHA results in the **FNMA** (Federal National Mortgage Association). Goal: to trigger more home buying and home construction by purchasing mortgages from banks and other lending institutions, thereby making them more willing and able to keep offering mortgages. The FNMA will be nicknamed Fannie Mae.

February 16

A new **Agricultural Adjustment Act** to further the government's mission to control agricultural prices and promote soil care by paying farmers not to produce certain commodities. Farmers will be paid from general tax revenues so the Triple A's new lease on life is SCOTUS-proof.

June 25

FLSA (Fair Labor Standards Act). Goal: to improve the quality of life for workers in the industrial sector. FLSA provisions include a federal minimum hourly wage (initially 25 cents) and a maximum workweek (initially 44 hours). FLSA also outlaws child labor in the industrial sector, something that had become permissible again with the demise of the NRA.

Hallie Flanagan in 1941.

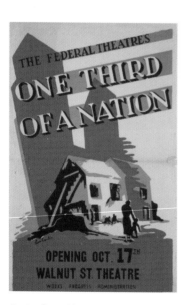

Poster for a Living Newspaper on housing. Other productions dealt with health care and lynching.

*R*oosevelt and *ruin?* many people now wondered. On top of being angry about the court-packing scheme and the Roosevelt Recession, a growing number of Americans were looking at the New Deal and seeing Red.

Texas representative Martin Dies was one. In the spring of 1938, Dies became chair of a congressional committee investigating subversive activities: HUAC (House Un-American Activities Committee).

HUAC saw communism as the main menace. New Deal–emboldened labor unions were top targets, especially those in the CIO, which did have CPUSA-spawned affiliates. Example: UCAPAWA (United Cannery, Agricultural, Packing, and Allied Workers of America).

ER, Harry Hopkins, Harold Ickes, and Frances Perkins were among the New Dealers rumored to be closet communists or communist sympathizers, with Perkins enduring an ultimately unsuccessful campaign for her impeachment.

HUAC also charged that New Deal agencies were infested with communists—especially the WPA arts programs, in particular the theater division.

Some productions that FTP chief Hallie Flanagan considered consciousness raisers were condemned by Martin Dies as attempts to foment revolution. FTP's alleged un-American activities included its Living Newspapers. There was also *The Cradle Will Rock,* a pro-union opera inspired by the 1937 strikes. Under pressure, the WPA had canceled *Cradle* before it opened.

Thanks to HUAC, it was curtains for the whole FTP in June 1939: Congress cut its funding.

*B*y the time the FTP was history, the dogs of war were howling, straining at the leash.

Starting in 1935, Congress had passed a neutrality act annually, pledging to stay out of other nations' fights. Since then

Italy had invaded Ethiopia, Japan had invaded China, and Spain had suffered a civil war and was now under the dictatorship of Generalissimo Francisco Franco.

Germany had been on a tear, too. Most recently, in the spring of 1939, it had taken Czechoslovakia.

A few months later, on September 1, at around three a.m., FDR got a chilling call: Hitler's soldiers had attacked Poland.

Two days later, Britain, then France, declared war on Germany.

That evening, FDR had a fireside chat.

Yes, the world was a storm, said the president.

No, the USA was not scrapping its commitment to neutrality.

Many Americans felt relieved. Others sensed that the nation had a rendezvous with war.

December 8, 1941: The latest news, at the corner of San Francisco's Montgomery and Market streets.

Like this sticker, the pins were in support of the GOP's 1940 presidential candidate: Wendell Willkie, a utilities executive and former Democrat.

GOOD DEAL?
RAW DEAL? MISDEAL?

While people disagree about what caused the Great Depression, there is consensus that the New Deal did not kick it out, but that World War II did.

The point of contention is, What kind of deal *was* the New Deal?

The New Deal gave birth to big government, generated a slew of regulations, put labor on the map, and created the American welfare state—that is, a nation that provides some citizens with safety nets.

These are just a few of the issues that arise in debates about whether the New Deal was a good deal, a raw deal, or a misdeal.

In the end, your take depends on your politics, your priorities, and your ideals—or, put another way, your answer to the question, What kind of government do you want?

" Only with trepidation will students of history try to judge the results of the New Deal. . . . But judge they must, not to whip the past but to use it. "

—Paul K. Conkin, *The New Deal* (1967).

" What the New Deal did was to refurbish middle-class America . . . to restore jobs to half the jobless, and to give just enough to the lowest classes . . . to create an aura of good will. "

—Howard Zinn, *New Deal Thought* (1966).

" The conclusion seems inescapable that . . . the New Deal . . . was truly a revolution in ideas, institutions and practices. "

—Carl N. Degler, *Out of Our Past* (1959).

1967: The suspension span of the PWA-funded Triborough Bridge, linking the Bronx, Manhattan, and Queens, New York. Opening day: July 11, 1936. In 2008, the bridge was renamed for one of President JFK's brothers, former U.S. attorney general and slain 1968 Democratic presidential hopeful RFK.

"Above all, the New Deal gave to countless Americans who had never had much of it a sense of security, and with it a sense of having a stake in their country. And it did it all without shredding the American Constitution or sundering the American people."

—David M. Kennedy, *Freedom from Fear* (1999).

"The liberal reforms of the New Deal did not transform the American system; they conserved and protected American corporate capitalism."

—Barton J. Bernstein, "The Conservative Achievement of New Deal Reform" (1968).

"From 1929 to 1940, from Hoover to Roosevelt, government intervention helped to make the Depression Great."

—Amity Shlaes, *The Forgotten Man* (2007).

"The New Deal . . . contributed a tremendous amount to the nation's public life in the form of physical and cultural infrastructure. . . . There was a time in our history when people found ways to combat despair by building for the future. The evidence is all around us."

—Robert D. Leighninger Jr., *Long-Range Public Investment* (2007).

"In fact, one could argue that if the actions of the Hundred Days had succeeded better and the positive economic trends of mid-1933 had brought full recovery in 1934 and 1935, the United States would not now have the wide variety of social advances that it largely takes for granted. The irony is that Roosevelt's failure to whip the Depression quickly may have been a blessing for future generations."

—Jonathan Alter, *The Defining Moment* (2006).

Postscript: The Fate of Some Alphabet Soup and Other New Deal Actions

1939

PWA (Public Works Administration) is abolished, having sponsored about 26,000 projects. They include more than 9,000 highways and streets, 7,000 educational buildings (elementary schools to colleges), 800 mental- and physical-health-care facilities, 600 city halls and courthouses, 350 airports, and 50 housing projects; many playgrounds, the Conservatory Garden, and the zoo in New York City's Central Park; Hoover (Boulder) and Grand Coulee dams, Denver's water supply system; Chicago's Outer Drive Bridge; San Francisco's Bay Bridge; Miami's Orange Bowl; and Washington National Airport (renamed in 1998 after President Ronald Reagan, whose father, Jack, and brother, Neil, had administrative jobs with the CWA).

REA (Rural Electrification Administration) becomes part of the **USDA** (United States Department of Agriculture).

Social Security now includes benefits to dependents of eligible retired and deceased workers (their young children, for example).

FSRC (Federal Surplus Relief Corporation), which became the **FSCC** (Federal Surplus Commodities Corporation) in 1935 when it was made part of the USDA, inspires a temporary-food-assistance program, the **FSP** (Food Stamp Program).

1942

FSA (Farm Security Administration) is abolished. It will best be remembered for the tens of thousands of documentary photographs of New Deal America taken by Jack Delano, Walker Evans, Dorothea Lange, Russell Lee, Gordon Parks, and other photographers on its (and the RA's) payroll.

1943

CCC (Civilian Conservation Corps) is abolished, having employed about 2.5 million people in roughly 80,000 projects. They include construction of about 46,000 bridges, 27,000 miles of fencing, 10,000 miles of roads and trails, 5,000 miles of water supply lines, and 3,000 fire lookout towers; the improvement and restoration of about 4,000 historic structures and 3,400 beaches; and the planting of 3 billion trees.

NYA (National Youth Administration) is abolished, having created job-training programs in an array of trades (carpentry, barbering, and baking, for example) and facilitated about 3 million private and public sector jobs (such as clerical workers, teacher's aides, nurse's aides, assistant librarians, museum guides, lifeguards, and apprentices in trades).

WPA (Works Progress Administration, renamed Works *Projects* Administration in 1939) is abolished, having generated some 8.5 million jobs in about 1.4 million projects. They include building, repairing, and refurbishing more than 600,000 miles of roads and streets, more than 120,000 public buildings (from schools to courthouses), and about 80,000 recreational facilities (from parks, pools, and playgrounds to gyms and golf courses, skating rinks and stadiums). Standout construction projects include San Antonio's River Walk and the presidential retreat Camp David (originally Camp Hi-Catoctin, for federal employees). The WPA's contributions to the cultural infrastructure include putting on more than 200,000 concerts and producing about 475,000 works of art.

1945

TVA (Tennessee Valley Authority) is the largest U.S. electricity supplier.

1947

Over **President Harry Truman's** veto, Congress passes the **Taft-Hartley Act,** which weakens the **Wagner Act.** Among other things, Taft-Hartley requires union officials to swear that they are not communists, outlaws the "closed shop" (the hiring of union members only), makes supervisors ineligible for union membership, and defines unfair labor practices— not for capital, but for labor (example: sympathy strikes). Also: the government can declare a strike illegal if it is deemed detrimental to the national interest.

1950

FDIC (Federal Deposit Insurance Corporation) coverage is raised from $5,000 to $10,000 and will see more increases in decades to come.

Social Security gets a COLA (cost-of-living adjustment), setting a precedent for future COLAs.

1956

President Dwight Eisenhower signs a bill that expands Social Security to include disability insurance.

1962

At the behest of **President JFK,** Congress enlarges the welfare system. It is no longer limited to widows with children, and so **ADC** (Aid to Dependent Children) becomes **AFDC** (Aid to Families with Dependent Children).

1964

President LBJ gets Congress to make the **FSP** permanent. Decades later, it will be renamed **SNAP** (Supplemental Nutrition Assistance Program). The USDA will continue to administer the program through its **FNS** (Food and Nutrition Service). The FNS's own alphabet soup will include **NSLP** (National School Lunch Program), **TEFAP** (The Emergency Food Assistance Program), and **WIC** (Women, Infants, and Children).

1965

As part of his War on Poverty and goal of making America a Great Society, **President LBJ** pushes for an expansion of the welfare system. New initiatives include **Medicare** (health care for seniors, attached to **Social Security**), **Medicaid** (health care for the poor), job-training programs (including the NYA-like **Neighborhood Youth Corps**), and the creation of **HUD** (Housing and Urban Development), into which the **FHA** (Federal Housing Administration) is folded.

1968

Fannie Mae (Federal National Mortgage Association) is changed from a government-owned to a shareholder-owned enterprise. **Ginnie Mae** (Government National Mortgage Association) is created to issue government-guaranteed mortgage-backed bonds. Fannie and Ginnie will soon get cousins: **Freddie Mac** (Federal Home Loan Mortgage Corporation), also in the mortgage-backed securities business, and the student loan provider **Sallie Mae** (Student Loan Marketing Association). Freddie and Sallie will start out as government agencies in the 1970s and, like Fannie, end up independent companies.

1974

By EO, **President Gerald Ford** lifts the ban on buying, selling, and owning gold. However, paying for goods and services with gold remains verboten.

1980

FDIC coverage is raised to $100,000.

1993

Houston-based Enron Corporation successfully petitions the **SEC** (Securities and Exchange Commission) for exemption from **PUHCA** (Public Utilities Holding Company Act) on the grounds that the company isn't really a utility but an energy marketer. Enron becomes a giant energy-trading and telecommunications company and master of accounting fraud, manifested in inflated stock prices, among other things. Enron will collapse in 2001.

1994

The **REA** is abolished and its work continued by the USDA's **RUS** (Rural Utilities Service). Utilities now include telephone service, among other things.

1996

President Bill Clinton signs into law **PRWORA** (Personal Responsibility and Work Opportunity Reconciliation Act). PRWORA places limits on the number of years a family can receive public assistance. **AFDC** becomes **TANF** (Temporary Assistance for Needy Families). In a 1994 statement on welfare reform, Clinton had said, "I believe we must end welfare as we know it, because the current welfare system is a bad deal for the taxpayers who pay the bills and for the families who are trapped on it." In his January 1996 State of the Union address, Clinton had declared that "the era of big Government is over."

1999

President Bill Clinton signs into law a bill repealing the part of the **Glass-Steagall Act** of 1933 that outlawed universal banks. Firms can now do both commercial and investment banking.

President George W. Bush signs into law the **Energy Policy Act**, which includes the repeal of **PUHCA.**

President George W. Bush ramps up his call for Social Security to be partially privatized, contending that people would be better off investing money in the stock market that otherwise would be taken out of their paychecks for Social Security. Congress, though, never acted on his proposal.

Fannie Mae and **Freddie Mac** are among several financial institutions Uncle Sam bails out because they are close to collapse and overburdened with debt, like so many other companies—and people at the top and bottom of the economic pyramid, and in between.

Amid bank failures and bank runs, Congress mandates a temporary increase to the **FDIC** guarantee, from $100,000 to $250,000.

Author's Note

The New Deal was very much in the news in 2008, initially because it was the seventy-fifth anniversary of FDR's historic First Hundred Days, the New Deal's start.

Then came the economic meltdown.

"Do you feel as if you're in a time warp?" That was a summer 2008 e-mail from Trish Parcell, who designed this book.

Trish and I had recently met for the first time and I was almost done with the last draft: revising the narrative, crafting captions, checking facts. When I found myself of two minds on a visual, I sounded out Trish; my first editor, Erin Clarke; and after Erin went on maternity leave, my second editor, Nancy Hinkel, with whom I would spend much time (in person, online, on the phone) going over passages that sagged or clunked or seemed TMI. And all of us were staying tuned to the whirlwind of terrible economic news.

Too many banks were failing. So many other types of businesses were going bust. Home foreclosures were mounting along with defaults on other loans—auto, student, credit cards. Legions were losing their jobs.

The party—obscene greed, materialism, debt addiction—was over.

And the stock market had been falling, falling, falling, wiping out trillions, turning millions of college, retirement, and other life plans into dust in the wind. Soon Ponzi schemes would pop and there'd be a sit-down strike in Chicago.

"Not since the Great Depression" was the catchphrase of many a day. And the meltdown was global.

Yes, I felt as if in a time warp.

Back in 2007 when I started this book, I told friends that I was seeing way too many parallels. Some thought me nuts, but I stuck with my gut, convinced that I was witnessing a paradigm shift.

While so much history was repeating (or rhyming), I was even more committed to hooking young people up on history, so that they might have more understanding of their twenty-first-century lives.

I had no plans to be comprehensive, but only to offer a starting point for exploring an ever-relevant era. What's more, I never thought to do a book for mere report writing, but rather for all the curious young minds that I know are out there, teens quite capable of reading a book cover to cover, teens who I felt could handle the soup perhaps better than members of my age group. After all, we didn't grow up using the likes of LOL and TTYL on the regular.

In the meantime, the news was schooling us all on another batch of alphabet soup. Example: TARP (Troubled Asset Relief Program), cooked up by then Treasury Secretary Hank Paulson. Goal: to commit $700 billion in taxpayer money to bail out insurance giant AIG (American International Group) and other financial institutions with toxic assets, whether an ABS (Asset-Backed Security), an MBS (Mortgage-Backed Security), a CDO (Collateralized Debt Obligation), a CMO (Collateralized Mortgage Obligation), a CBO (Collateralized Bond Obligation), a CDS (Credit Default Swap), or some other bet gone bad.

And it was at such a time as this, when all hell was breaking loose, that Americans elected as president a person of undisputed black African descent.

Come Inauguration Day 2009, millions were on tiptoe, some hoping, others fearing, that President Barack Hussein Obama would pledge himself to a new New Deal for the American people.

We would watch and see, just as people did during the days of FDR.

1940: Americans not only got FDR
again in 1940 but also in 1944.

Glossary

This glossary defines initialisms, acronyms, and terms as they are used in this book.

A

AAA: Agricultural Adjustment Administration.

ACLU: American Civil Liberties Union, formed in 1920 to promote liberty and justice for all kinds of people.

ADC: Aid to Dependent Children, established 1935; renamed **AFDC** (Aid to Families with Dependent Children) in 1962, then **TANF** (Temporary Assistance for Needy Families) in 1996.

AFDC: Aid to Families with Dependent Children.

AFL: American Federation of Labor, a union of unions.

AICP: Association for Improving the Condition of the Poor, a charitable organization in New York City.

aka: also known as.

American Liberty League: an organization of anti–New Deal activists. Most were industrialists and financiers.

B

BEP: Bureau of Engraving and Printing.

Black Cabinet: a group of federal employees with whom FDR sometimes consulted on issues important to black America.

blue-collar: pertaining to manual labor, which is usually paid by the hour.

Bonus Army: informal name for WWI vets who marched on Washington in 1932 for early release of their pensions, which they called a bonus. The group's official name was Bonus Expeditionary Force, a takeoff on the name of U.S. armed forces in Europe during WWI: the American Expeditionary Force.

bootleg: describing illegal alcoholic beverages, or any ill-gotten goods.

brain trust: a group of advisers.

breadline: a line of people outside a charity giving out free food, usually more than bread and often soup.

broker: the go-between in the buying and selling of securities.

C

capitalism: a socioeconomic and political system in which individuals own the means of production (like auto plants and farms), and the free market—that is, the law of supply and demand—determines wages and prices for goods and services. Laissez-faire capitalism calls for government to pretty much stay out of business's business. (*Laissez-faire* is French for "allow to do" or "leave alone.")

CAWIU: Cannery and Agricultural Workers Industrial Union.

CCC: Civilian Conservation Corps.

CIO: originally Committee for Industrial Organization when part of the **AFL,** then Congress of Industrial Organizations after it split with the AFL in 1938 and became a separate union for **industrial unions.** In 1955, the AFL and CIO formally merged to form the AFL-CIO.

COLA: cost-of-living adjustment.

commercial bank: a bank in the principal business of handling deposit accounts and making loans.

communism: a socioeconomic and political system in which people, collectively, own the means of production. Individuals contribute to society what they can and receive from society what they need.

concentration of wealth: unequal distribution of resources, so that a few people possess and control the lion's share of the wealth. Causes include paying rank-and-file workers wages that do not keep up with rises in the cost of living while giving CEOs exorbitant salaries and bonuses, along with tax laws that favor the wealthy.

CPUSA: Communist Party USA, formed in 1919 by radical members of the **SPA.**

CWA: Civil Works Administration.

D

deflation: a drop in the prices of goods and services, often triggered by a drop in spending, and leading to job losses. Also, a decrease of the money supply.

Democratic National Committee: the organization that manages the Democratic Party, handling its day-to-day business (from fundraising to public relations).

Dems: slang for members of the Democratic Party.

dole, the: government assistance.

E

EO: executive order, a decree to the government from the president, a governor, or other executive authority.

EPIC: End Poverty in California.

ER: Eleanor Roosevelt, born Anna Eleanor Roosevelt.

F

Fannie Mae: nickname for the Federal National Mortgage Association **(FNMA).**

FAP: Federal Art Project, a division of the **WPA's** public arts program, officially Federal Project Number One.

fascism: a socioeconomic and political system in which the government dictates all manner of things, from how businesses should function to how people should think.

FBI: Federal Bureau of Investigation.

FCA: Farm Credit Administration.

FCC: Federal Communications Commission.

FCS: Farm Credit System.

FDIC: Federal Deposit Insurance Corporation.

FDR: Franklin Delano Roosevelt.

Fed, the: shorthand for the Federal Reserve System, the U.S. central bank.

FERA: Federal Emergency Relief Administration.

FFMC: Federal Farm Mortgage Corporation.

FHA: Federal Housing Administration.

fiat money: money made legal tender by government decree. *Fiat* comes from the Latin for "let it be done."

financial institution: a firm that deals with money, from holding it for individuals and firms to making (and losing) it for individuals and firms. A financial institution might be a **commercial bank,** a credit union, an **investment bank,** a retail bank, a savings bank, an S&L (savings and loan association, dealing mostly in savings accounts and mortgage lending), or a **universal bank.**

fireside chat: an informal talk to the nation, originally only by radio.

First Hundred Days: March 9 to June 16, 1933, during which time FDR pushed for and made an unprecedented number of laws to advance his agenda for the nation. Since then, people have often judged presidents by what they accomplish during their first hundred days in office.

fiscal: having to do with government debt, spending, and revenue.

FMP: Federal Music Project, a division of the **WPA**'s public arts program, officially Federal Project Number One.

FNMA: Federal National Mortgage Association, aka **Fannie Mae.**

FNS: Food and Nutrition Service, part of the **USDA.**

FOR: Fellowship of Reconciliation, a human rights organization founded in England in 1914. Its American branch, FOR-USA, was founded a year later.

Freddie Mac: nickname for the Federal Home Loan Mortgage Corporation (FHLMC).

FSA: Farm Security Administration, successor to the **RA.**

FSCC: Federal Surplus Commodities Corporation (formerly **FSRC**).

FSP: Food Stamp Program, renamed SNAP in 2008: Supplemental Nutrition Assistance Program.

FSRC: Federal Surplus Relief Corporation.

FTP: Federal Theatre Project, a division of the **WPA**'s public arts program, officially Federal Project Number One.

FWP: Federal Writers' Project, a division of the **WPA**'s public arts program, officially Federal Project Number One.

G

Ginnie Mae: nickname for the Government National Mortgage Association (GNMA).

Glass-Steagall Act of 1933: a banking act that included a ban on the **universal bank.**

GM: General Motors Corporation.

GMAC: General Motors Acceptance Corporation. The division of GM that's in the credit business.

G-man: slang for an **FBI** agent, short for "government man."

gold standard: a monetary system in which currency is backed by a specific amount of gold.

GOP: nickname for the Republican Party. "GOP" has stood for "Gallant Old Party" and "Grand Old Party," among other things.

H

hobo jungle: an encampment of homeless people, many of whom lived off the grid even during prosperous times.

HOLC: Home Owners' Loan Corporation.

Hooverville: a makeshift "neighborhood" (often on dumpsites and vacant land). Most residents of Hoovervilles—so named after President Herbert Hoover—had become homeless because they lost their jobs.

HUAC: House Un-American Activities Committee.

HUD: Housing and Urban Development.

hyperinflation: runaway inflation.

I

ILA: International Longshoremen's Association, a labor union.

ILD: International Labor Defense, the legal wing of the **CPUSA.**

ILGWU: International Ladies' Garment Workers' Union, formed in 1900. In the 1990s, it merged with ACTWU (Amalgamated Clothing and Textile Workers Union) to form UNITE (Union of Needletrades, Industrial and Textile Employees).

industrial union: a union organizing workers throughout an entire industry, such as publishing, regardless of their specific craft or level of skill. By contrast, a craft union organizes skilled workers with a specific craft, such as writing or copyediting.

inflation: a rise in prices of goods and services, usually without a fully equivalent rise in wages. Also, an increase in the money supply.

in the black: having more income than outgo.

investment bank: a bank that sells securities to the government and to other businesses. An investment bank may also handle M&As (mergers and acquisitions).

J

JFK: John Fitzgerald Kennedy.

Jim Crow: racial segregation.

K

KKK: Ku Klux Klan, a white supremacist terrorist militia formed after the Civil War.

L

LBJ: Lyndon Baines Johnson.

Left, the: shorthand for people committed to liberal, progressive, radical, or antiestablishment politics and ideologies. See **Right, the.** Origin: the seating arrangement in France's Assembly around the time of the French Revolution. Members for the status quo sat on the right; the opposition, on the left.

M

MGM: Metro-Goldwyn-Mayer, a Hollywood movie studio.

MOMA: Museum of Modern Art.

monetary: pertaining to actual money, including currency and coin and their supply.

MSG: Madison Square Garden.

N

NAACP: National Association for the Advancement of Colored People, a civil and human rights organization founded in 1909 by a mostly white group of lawyers, professors, social workers, and other professionals, many of whom were socialists.

NCNW: National Council of Negro Women, an umbrella organization of civic groups.

NCUC: National Committee of Unemployed Councils USA, a **CPUSA** advocate for the jobless.

NIRA: National Industrial Recovery Act of 1933.

NLB: National Labor Board.

NRA: National Recovery Administration.

NSLP: National School Lunch Program, part of **FNS.**

NUSJ: National Union for Social Justice, founded by Father Charles "the Radio Priest" Coughlin.

NYA: National Youth Administration, a division of the **WPA.**

O

OARP: Old Age Revolving Pension, the official name of the **Townsend Plan.**

P

POTUS: president of the United States.

presidential proclamation: a decree to the public at large.

Prohibition: the period when, with the exception of some medicinal purposes, booze was banned in America. The Eighteenth Amendment (January 1919) outlawed the making, selling, and transportation of alcohol. The

National Prohibition Act, aka the Volstead Act (October 1919), gave law enforcement the power to go after people who violated the Eighteenth Amendment. National Prohibition was ended by the Twenty-first Amendment in December 1933.

PRWORA: Personal Responsibility and Work Opportunity Reconciliation Act.

PUHCA: Public Utilities Holding Company Act.

PWA: Public Works Administration.

Q

q.t., on the: on the quiet.

R

RA: Resettlement Administration.

REA: Rural Electrification Administration.

Red: a derogatory name for people and ideas associated with **communism.**

reflation: monetary policies a government employs to stop deflation and stimulate the economy. Also, getting more money into circulation.

Republican National Committee: aka the RNC, the outfit that manages the Republican Party, handling its day-to-day business (from fund-raising to public relations).

RFC: Reconstruction Finance Corporation.

RFK: Robert Francis Kennedy.

Right, the: shorthand for people committed to conservative politics and ideologies. See **Left, the.**

RKO: Radio-Keith-Orpheum Pictures, a Hollywood movie studio.

RUS: Rural Utilities Service.

S

Sallie Mae: nickname for the Student Loan Marketing Association (SLMA).

SBP: School Breakfast Program, part of **FNS.**

SCOTUS: Supreme Court of the United States.

screwball comedy: a fast-paced, LOL film whose plot involves courtship or marriage.

SEC: Securities and Exchange Commission, Wall Street's watchdog.

Section 7(a): the section of the **NIRA** that was regarded as labor's bill of rights.

secured loan: a loan that is backed by something the borrower owns (collateral), like a house. If the borrower fails to repay the loan as agreed, the lender may take possession of the collateral.

securities: financial investments, which include stocks (shares or a piece of the action in a company) and bonds (a piece of the action in a large, interest-paying loan).

She, She, She: a derisive nickname for a work relief program for young women modeled on the **CCC.**

socialism: a socioeconomic and political system in which people, collectively, own the major means of production. What individuals receive from society is based on what those individuals contribute. (The industrious can make more money than the lazy.)

SOW: Share Our Wealth, a society founded by Louisiana senator Huey Long.

SPA: Socialist Party of America, born in 1901 from a merger of Eugene V. Debs's Social Democratic Party and less radical members of the oldest U.S. socialist party, the SLP (Socialist Labor Party).

stagflation: stagnation plus **inflation.**

stagnation: lack of, or very slow, economic growth, accompanied by rising unemployment.

STFU: Southern Tenant Farmers' Union.

SWOC: Steel Workers Organizing Committee, a seed union of the USW (United Steelworkers).

T

TANF: Temporary Assistance for Needy Families.

TEFAP: The Emergency Food Assistance Program, part of **FNS.**

TERA: New York State's Temporary Emergency Relief Administration.

Townsend Plan: informal name of **OARP.**

TR: Theodore "Teddy" Roosevelt.

Treasury: shorthand for the United States Department of the Treasury, the manufacturer of U.S. currency and coin, collector of money owed to the government, and payer of the government's debts.

Tree Army: nickname for the **CCC.**

troy ounce: a unit of weight used for gold and other precious metals. One troy ounce is equal to about 1.1 avoirdupois ounces.

TVA: Tennessee Valley Authority.

two bits: a quarter dollar.

U

UAW: originally United Automobile Workers. While keeping the same initialism, the union expanded. Its full name is the International Union, United Automobile, Aerospace and Agricultural Implement Workers of America.

UCAPAWA: United Cannery, Agricultural, Packing, and Allied Workers of America.

UMW: United Mine Workers of America.

Uncle Sam: nickname for the U.S. government. Also the image of a man personifying the U.S. government (a gaunt fellow with a goatee, usually dressed in red, white, and blue, sporting a top hat, and pointing a finger at you).

universal bank: a bank that engages in both commercial and investment banking.

USDA: United States Department of Agriculture.

USHA: United States Housing Authority.

UTW: United Textile Workers. In the late 1930s, this union became the TWU (Textile Workers Union), then, decades later, merged with the Amalgamated Clothing Workers of America to form the ACTWU (Amalgamated Clothing and Textile Workers Union).

V

verboten: forbidden, borrowed from German.

VP: vice president.

W

Wagner Act: informal name for the National Labor Relations Act, regarded as labor's Magna Carta.

Wall Street: NYC's financial district and a symbol of the U.S. financial industry at large.

want creation: a way of boosting consumption of non-essentials, usually through advertising.

welfare: government assistance to people in need. The word comes from the Middle English *wel faren,* meaning "to fare well." Government aid to big business—tax breaks and bailouts, for example—is often called "corporate welfare."

white-collar: pertaining to work that typically doesn't require physical labor and for which one receives a salary.

WIC: Women, Infants, and Children, part of **FNS.**

wildcat strike: a strike not authorized by union leadership.

WPA: originally Works Progress Administration, renamed Works Projects Administration.

Notes

All Web sites and links cited here were up and active when this book was published.

EPIGRAPH

"In a game . . .": Southworth and Southworth, *The New Deal: An Impartial History*, 1.

1: BROKE AND HUNGRY

On Albert Sacks: Associated Press, "Freed Convict Begs to Return to Prison," *Detroit Free Press*, July 3, 1932. My search for more information on Albert Sacks's second stint at Auburn State Prison ended in disappointment. The prison referred me to the New York State Archives, which reported: "Apparently his files, like the files of many other inmates from the early 20th century, were destroyed while the records were still in custody of the NYS Department of Correctional Services."

On stock market losses: Lopus, "The Stock Market Crashes of 1929 and 1987," *Social Education*, 71.

On bank failures: Kennedy, *Freedom from Fear*, 163; Wheelock, "An Overview of the Great Depression."

On savings losses: FDIC Learning Bank, www.fdic.gov/about/learn/learning/when/1930s.html.

On business failures: Watkins, *The Hungry Years*, 43.

On unemployment: Friedrich, "FDR's Disputed Legacy," *Time*, February 1, 1982.

On home foreclosures: Kennedy, *Freedom from Fear*, 163.

On farm income: McElvaine, *Down and Out in the Great Depression*, 27.

On national income: Friedrich, "FDR's Disputed Legacy," *Time*, February 1, 1982.

On suicides: Watkins, *The Hungry Years*, 54.

"The duty of . . . *social duty*": P. Smith, *Redeeming the Time*, 379.

"the forgotten man . . .": Alter, *The Defining Moment*, 90.

"The country needs . . . try something": F. D. Roosevelt, "Address at Oglethorpe University, May 22, 1932."

"Our president is . . .": Dickson and Allen, *The Bonus Army*, 49.

On concentration of wealth: Frank, "Wealth Gap Is Focus Even as It Shrinks," *Wall Street Journal*, October 27, 2008.

On Smoot-Hawley: This act is also known as Hawley-Smoot.

FDR's 1932 acceptance speech: Ciment, *Encyclopedia of the Great Depression and the New Deal*, 725–30.

2: KICK OUT DEPRESSION

On the Bonus Army's letdown: Congress did appropriate $100,000 to pay for vets' travel expenses home. The money was a loan that would be deducted from the eventual bonus pay if not repaid.

"Stay at Home—Buy Nothing—Sell Nothing": Watkins, *The Hungry Years*, 348.

"Mr. Licht at the Welfare . . .": Ibid., 110.

On NCUC demands: NCUC, *Poverty 'Midst Riches*, 9–10, 40. Presented to Congress by the historic National Hunger March on December 7, 1931, and read into Senate record, December 30, 1931.

"To bring on . . ." and **"If I vote . . .":** Alter, *The Defining Moment*, 82, 83.

"20,000 Reds Demand . . .": "20,000 Reds Demand a 'Soviet America,'" *New York Times*, November 7, 1932.

"Communist Party fights . . ." and **"in city after city . . .":** Cunard, *Negro*, 144.

"Hoover program of . . . hatred against Hoover": "20,000 Reds Demand a 'Soviet America,'" *New York Times*, November 7, 1932.

"If you vote . . . glorified racketeering": "11,000 Hear Thomas in Socialist Wind-Up," *New York Times*, November 7, 1932.

On the bill Hoover signed in July 1932: Kennedy, *Freedom from Fear*, 91.

"so-called new deals . . .": The American Presidency Project, www.presidency.ucsb.edu/ws/index.php?pid=23317.

On election returns: "Historical Statistics of the U.S.," 1,073.

"Many essential public . . .": Rauchway, *The Great Depression and the New Deal*, 42–43.

3: ALPHABET SOUP

"Will he make . . .": "Man of the Year," *Time*, January 2, 1933.

"When I am . . .": Picchi, *The Five Weeks of Giuseppe Zangara*, 117.

"Viva Italia! . . . pusha da button!": Ibid., 191.

FDR's first inaugural address: Ciment, *Encyclopedia of the Great Depression and the New Deal*, 752–54.

"The lobby of . . .": Leuchtenburg, *The New Deal: A Documentary History*, 19.

On foreclosures: Wheelock, "The Federal Response to Home Mortgage Distress," 138.

On bank failures: Watkins, *The Hungry Years*, 150.

"Of course we . . .": Leuchtenburg, *Franklin D. Roosevelt and the New Deal*, 30.

"This is Chapter 1 . . . Federal Government": Leuchtenburg, *The New Deal: A Documentary History*, 25.

On Emergency Banking Act: It's also known as the Emergency Banking Relief Act.

"The president wants . . .": Alter, *The Defining Moment*, 264.

FDR's March 12, 1933, fireside chat: Ciment, *Encyclopedia of the Great Depression and the New Deal*, 754–56.

"Of course, it is . . .": Badger, *FDR: The First Hundred Days*, 40–41.

FDR's July 24, 1933, fireside chat: Ciment, *Encyclopedia of the Great Depression and the New Deal*, 763–64.

"It was homey . . .": Alter, *The Defining Moment*, 270.

"I tried to picture . . .": Ibid., 266.

"What I want . . .": Lowitt and Beasley, *One Third of a Nation*, ix–x.

"I don't want . . ." and **"Yes, I'll back you":** Berg, "Frances Perkins and the Flowering of Economic and Social Policies," *Monthly Labor Review*, 1989.

"I Want You to Write to Me": E. Roosevelt, *Woman's Home Companion*, August 1933, 4.

"It looks as . . .": "Alphabet Soup," *Time*, December 11, 1933.

On tax revenue: Badger, *FDR: The First Hundred Days*, 53.

"Will you please . . .": McElvaine, *Down and Out in the Great Depression*, 149–50.

4: IS ROOSEVELT GOING SOCIALIST?

"Nineteen hundred and . . . a socialistic commonwealth": Franklin, "Is Roosevelt Going Socialist?" *Liberty*, March 10, 1934, 5.

On 1934 deficit: Ciment, *Encyclopedia of the Great Depression and the New Deal*, 306.

On CWA projects: Leighninger, *Long-Range Public Investment*, 51.

"There was something . . .": Watkins, *The Hungry Years*, 173.

"State socialism" and "No Recovery Allowed": Allen, *Since Yesterday*, 162.

"Negro Run Around" and "Negroes Ruined Again": Sitkoff, *A New Deal for Blacks*, 55.

"I was always . . .": Watkins, *The Hungry Years*, 197.

"THE PRESIDENT WANTS . . .": Watkins, *The Hungry Years*, 216.

Section 7(a): Ciment, *Encyclopedia of the Great Depression and the New Deal*, 686.

On ILGWU membership: Ibid., 220; Galenson, *The CIO Challenge to the AFL*, 300.

"Set a thief . . .": J. E. Smith, *FDR*, 346 (footnote).

FDR's June 28, 1934, fireside chat: The American Presidency Project, www.presidency.ucsb.edu/ws/index.php?pid=14703.

C.L.F.'s letter: McElvaine, *Down and Out in the Great Depression*, 223.

"Shorter hours! Higher . . .": Watkins, *The Hungry Years*, 237.

5: CRACKPOT IDEAS?

"For more than . . .": Shouse, "Why? The American Liberty League," 2.

"Five Negroes on . . .": "The Carpenter and Raskob Letters," *New York Times*, December 21, 1934.

"while the [conservative Democrats] . . .": Franklin, "Is Roosevelt Going Socialist?" *Liberty*, March 10, 1934, 7.

"to secure better living . . .": "Southern Tenant Farmers Union Was Response to Unfair Labor Practices," Arkansas State University news release, September 22, 2006.

"What you need," "barely fit for pigs," and "Prosperity through starvation": Watkins, *The Hungry Years*, 382, 383.

"We colored people . . .": Shapiro, *White Violence and Black Response*, 238.

Long's February 1934 radio address: Ciment, *Encyclopedia of the Great Depression and the New Deal*, 760–62.

On median family income: Kennedy, *Freedom from Fear*, 238.

"Roosevelt or Ruin!" and "The New Deal is Christ's Deal": Brinkley, *Voices of Protest*, 108.

"I believe in . . .": Ibid., 287.

On Coughlin's listenership: J. E. Smith, *FDR*, 348."

Sirs: The Man . . .": "Letters," *Time*, December 17, 1934.

"A torrent of invectives . . . whole country hears!": Brinkley, *Voices of Protest*, 222–23.

"crackpot ideas": Kennedy, *Freedom from Fear*, 242.

Mrs. F.E.G.'s letter: McElvaine, *Down and Out in the Great Depression*, 103–4.

"Entering the Winter . . .": Lowitt and Beasley, *One Third of a Nation*, 357–58, 363, 364.

6: THE "SECOND NEW DEAL"

FDR's January 1935 State of the Union: The American Presidency Project, www.presidency.ucsb.edu/ws/?pid=14890.

"Big Bill": Kennedy, *Freedom from Fear*, 249.

11% of farms: J. E. Smith, *FDR*, 357.

"for children who . . .": Ciment, *Encyclopedia of the Great Depression and the New Deal*, 697.

M.S.'s letter: Cohen, *Dear Mrs. Roosevelt*, 46.

"wealth tax," "Amen!" "soak the rich," on tax rates, and "stealing Huey Long's thunder": Kennedy, *Freedom from Fear*, 275, 276, and Badger, *The New Deal*, 103.

"Huey Long is . . .": Brinkley, *Voices of Protest*, 198.

"If the Senate . . .": Posted at www. ssa.gov/history/fdrstmts.html#signing.

"We put those . . . social security program": Watkins, *The Hungry Years*, 258.

"There is no reason . . . security insurance system": Kennedy, *Freedom from Fear*, 262.

Battalion of Death: Kennedy, *Freedom from Fear*, 263. New Dealers also called the archconservative justices the Four Horsemen, a reference to the purveyors of death and destruction in the Bible.

Letter from Reidsville, Georgia: McElvaine, *Down and Out in the Great Depression*, 83.

"Hell, they've got . . .": Kennedy, *Freedom from Fear*, 254.

New Deal stats: J. E. Smith, *FDR*, 360–61; Kennedy, *Freedom from Fear*, 285.

"Theatre, when it is good . . . ," "All of this music . . . ," and "Art should belong . . .": Bindas, *All of This Music*, xii, xiii.

"I might not . . .": O'Connor and Brown, *Free, Adult, Uncensored*, 4.

"There is plenty . . .": Alsberg, *American Stuff*, vi.

"You know a hungry . . .": McElvaine, *Down and Out in the Great Depression*, 25–26.

7: RENDEZVOUS WITH DESTINY

Fortune poll: J. E. Smith, *FDR*, 361.

"I am fighting . . . the capitalist system": Kennedy, *Freedom from Fear*, 242.

FDR's 1936 acceptance speech: The American Presidency Project, www.presidency.ucsb.edu/ws/index.php?pid=15314.

On 1932 and 1936 returns: The American Presidency Project, www.presidency.ucsb.edu/showelection.php?year=1932; www.presidency.ucsb.edu/showelection.php?year=1936; J. E. Smith, *FDR*, 374, 731.

FDR's second inaugural address: Ciment, *Encyclopedia of the Great Depression and the New Deal*, 781–83.

On UMW's contributions: Kennedy, *Freedom from Fear*, 290.

"Roosevelt is the . . .": Irwin, "Does John L. Lewis Want to Be President?" *Liberty*, December 5, 1936, 7.

"We must capitalize . . .": Kennedy, *Freedom from Fear*, 290.

Data on GM: J. E. Smith, *FDR*, 394.

"Flint workers had . . .": Watkins, *The Hungry Years*, 324.

"Is that you, Bill?": J. E. Smith, *FDR*, 394.

On UAW membership: Kennedy, *Freedom from Fear*, 314.

On photo of Battle of the Overpass: There are several shots of this moment. Some show the figure at the far right in part, in full, or not at all.

On FDR's disgust with both labor and capital: Ibid., 319.

8: ROOSEVELT *AND* RUIN?

"Justice McReynolds will . . .": J. E. Smith, *FDR*, 381.

"A liberal cause . . .": Ibid., 384.

"I did not choose . . . take that risk": Sitkoff, *A New Deal for Blacks*, 46.

On job losses: Watkins, *The Hungry Years*, 505.

Ickes's radio address: "Text of Address by Secretary Ickes on 'It Is Happening Here,'" *New York Times*, December 31, 1937.

9: GOOD DEAL? RAW DEAL? MISDEAL?

"Only with trepidation . . .": Conkin, *The New Deal*, 106.

"What the New Deal . . .": Zinn, *New Deal Thought*, xvi.

"The conclusion seems . . .": Degler, *Out of Our Past*, 449.

"Above all, the New Deal . . .": Kennedy, *Freedom from Fear*, 379.

"The liberal reforms . . .": Bernstein, "The Conservative Achievement of New Deal Reform," in Hamilton, *The New Deal*, 19.

"From 1929 to 1940 . . .": Shlaes, *The Forgotten Man*, 90.

"In fact, one . . .": Alter, *The Defining Moment*, 274.

"The New Deal . . . contributed . . .": Leighninger, *Long-Range Public Investment*, 218.

POSTSCRIPT

On numbers for projects and employment: My main source was Leighninger, *Long-Range Public Investment*.

"I believe we . . .": "Statement on the White House Initiative on Welfare Reform," posted at The American Presidency Project, www.presidency.ucsb.edu/ws/index .php?pid=49565.

"the era of big . . .": "Address Before a Joint Session of the Congress on the State of the Union," posted at The American Presidency Project, www.presidency.ucsb.edu/ws/ index.php?pid=53091.

Selected Sources

Allen, Frederick Lewis. *Since Yesterday: The 1930s in America, September 3, 1929–September 3, 1939.* New York: Harper & Row, 1986.

Alsberg, Henry G., ed. *American Stuff: An Anthology of Prose and Verse by Members of the Federal Writers' Project.* New York: Viking, 1937.

Alter, Jonathan. *The Defining Moment: FDR's Hundred Days and the Triumph of Hope.* New York: Simon & Schuster, 2007.

Arkansas State University. "Southern Tenant Farmers Union Was Response to Unfair Labor Practices." News release, September 22, 2006. http://asunews.astate.edu/STFUlabor.htm.

Associated Press. "Freed Convict Begs to Return to Prison." *Detroit Free Press,* July 3, 1932.

Badger, Anthony J. *FDR: The First Hundred Days.* New York: Hill and Wang, 2008.

———. *The New Deal: The Depression Years, 1933–1940.* Chicago: Ivan R. Dee, 2002.

Bennett, G. H., ed. *Roosevelt's Peacetime Administrations, 1933–41: A Documentary History of the New Deal Years.* Manchester and New York: Manchester University Press, 2004.

Berg, Gordon. "Frances Perkins and the Flowering of Economic and Social Policies." *Monthly Labor Review,* vol. 112, no. 6, 1989. www.bls.gov/opub/mlr/1989/06/art5full.pdf.

Bindas, Kenneth J. *All of This Music Belongs to the Nation: The WPA's Federal Music Project and American Society, 1935–1939.* Knoxville: University of Tennessee Press, 1995.

Brinkley, Alan. *Voices of Protest: Huey Long, Father Coughlin, and the Great Depression.* New York: Vintage, 1983.

Ciment, James, ed. *Encyclopedia of the Great Depression and the New Deal.* 2 vols. Armonk, N.Y.: Sharpe, 2001.

Cohen, Robert. *Dear Mrs. Roosevelt: Letters from Children of the Great Depression.* Chapel Hill: University of North Carolina Press, 2002.

Conkin, Paul K. *The New Deal,* 3rd ed. Wheeling, Ill.: Harlan Davidson, 1992.

Cunard, Nancy, ed. *Negro: An Anthology.* New York: Frederick Ungar, 1984.

Degler, Carl N. "The Third American Revolution." In *Out of Our Past: The Forces That Shaped Modern America,* 3rd ed. New York: HarperCollins, 1983.

Dickson, Paul, and Thomas B. Allen. *The Bonus Army: An American Epic*. New York: Walker, 2004.

Flynn, Kathryn A., with Richard Polese. *The New Deal: A 75th Anniversary Celebration*. Layton, Utah: Gibbs Smith, 2008.

Frank, Robert. "Wealth Gap Is Focus Even as It Shrinks." *Wall Street Journal*, October 27, 2008. http://online.wsj.com/article/SB122506174552170247.html.

Franklin, Jay. "Is Roosevelt Going Socialist?" *Liberty*, March 10, 1934, 5–7.

Friedrich, Otto. "FDR's Disputed Legacy." *Time*, February 1, 1982. www.time.com/time/magazine/article/0,9171,954983,00.html.

Galenson, Walter. *The CIO Challenge to the AFL: A History of the American Labor Movement, 1935–1941*. Cambridge, Mass.: Harvard University Press, 1960.

Hamilton, David E., ed. *The New Deal*. Boston: Houghton Mifflin, 1999.

Irwin, Will. "Does John L. Lewis Want to Be President?" *Liberty*, December 5, 1936, 6–8.

Kennedy, David M. *Freedom from Fear: The American People in Depression and War, 1929–1945*. New York: Oxford University Press, 2005.

Leighninger, Robert D., Jr. *Long-Range Public Investment: The Forgotten Legacy of the New Deal*. Columbia: University of South Carolina Press, 2007.

Leuchtenburg, William E. *Franklin D. Roosevelt and the New Deal, 1932–1940*. New York: Harper Torchbooks, 1963.

———, ed. *The New Deal: A Documentary History*. New York: Harper Torchbooks, 1968.

Lopus, Jane S. "The Stock Market Crashes of 1929 and 1987: Linking History and Personal Finance Education." *Social Education*, vol. 69, no. 2, pp. 70–73, March 2005. http://members.ncss.org/se/6902/6902070.pdf.

Lowitt, Richard, and Maurine Beasley, eds. *One Third of a Nation: Lorena Hickok Reports on the Great Depression*. Urbana and Chicago: University of Illinois Press, 2000.

McElvaine, Robert S., ed. *Down and Out in the Great Depression: Letters from the Forgotten Man*. Chapel Hill: University of North Carolina Press, 1983.

NCUC. *Poverty 'Midst Riches*. December 7, 1931.

New York Times. "The Carpenter and Raskob Letters," December 21, 1934. www.nytimes.com/ref/membercenter/nytarchive.html.

———. "11,000 Hear Thomas in Socialist Wind-Up," November 7, 1932. www.nytimes.com/ref/membercenter/nytarchive.html.

———. "20,000 Reds Demand a 'Soviet America,'" November 7, 1932. www.nytimes.com/ref/membercenter/nytarchive.html.

———. "Text of Address by Secretary Ickes on 'It Is Happening Here.'" December 31, 1937. www.nytimes.com/ref/membercenter/nytarchive.html.

O'Connor, John, and Lorraine Brown, eds. *Free, Adult, Uncensored: The Living History of the Federal Theatre Project*. Washington, D.C.: New Republic, 1978.

Picchi, Blaise. *The Five Weeks of Giuseppe Zangara: The Man Who Would Assassinate FDR*. Chicago: Academy Chicago, 1998.

Powell, Jim. *FDR's Folly: How Roosevelt and His New Deal Prolonged the Great Depression*. New York: Three Rivers Press, 2003.

Rauchway, Eric. *The Great Depression and the New Deal: A Very Short Introduction.* New York: Oxford University Press, 2008.

Roosevelt, Eleanor. "I Want You to Write to Me." *Woman's Home Companion,* vol. 60, p. 4, August 1933. http://newdeal.feri.org/er/er01.htm.

Roosevelt, Franklin D. "Address at Oglethorpe University, May 22, 1932." http://newdeal. feri.org/speeches/1932d.htm.

Shapiro, Herbert. *White Violence and Black Response: From Reconstruction to Montgomery.* Amherst: University of Massachusetts Press, 1988.

Shlaes, Amity. *The Forgotten Man: A New History of the Great Depression.* New York: HarperCollins, 2007.

Shouse, Jouett. "Why? The American Liberty League." Washington, D.C.: American Liberty League, 1934. www.uky.edu/Libraries/images/Shouse/shouse-all-why.gif and www.uky.edu/Libraries/images/Shouse/shouse-all-why2.gif.

Sitkoff, Harvard. *A New Deal for Blacks: The Emergence of Civil Rights as a National Issue.* Vol. 1, *The Depression Decade.* New York: Oxford University Press, 1981.

Smith, Jean Edward. *FDR.* New York: Random House, 2007.

Smith, Page. *Redeeming the Time: A People's History of the 1920s and the New Deal.* New York: Penguin, 1991.

Southworth, Gertrude Van Duyn, and John Van Duyn Southworth. *The New Deal: An Impartial History of the Roosevelt Administration.* Syracuse, N.Y.: Iroquois, 1935.

Taylor, Nick. *American-Made: The Enduring Legacy of the WPA: When FDR Put the Nation to Work.* New York: Bantam, 2008.

Time. "Man of the Year," January 2, 1933.

———. "Alphabet Soup," December 11, 1933.

———. "Letters," December 17, 1934.

U.S. government. "Historical Statistics of the U.S.: From Colonial Times to 1970." Washington, D.C.: U.S. Bureau of Commerce, 1975.

Wasik, John F. *The Merchant of Power: Sam Insull, Thomas Edison, and the Creation of the Modern Metropolis.* New York: Palgrave Macmillan, 2006.

Watkins, T. H. *The Hungry Years: A Narrative History of the Great Depression in America.* New York: Owl, 2000.

Wheelock, David C. "An Overview of the Great Depression." Federal Reserve Bank of St. Louis, September 20, 2007. http://stlouisfed.org/greatdepression/resources/GreatDepression.ppt.

———. "The Federal Response to Home Mortgage Distress: Lessons from the Great Depression." Federal Reserve Bank of St. Louis *Review,* May/June 2008, 133–48. http://research.stlouisfed.org/publications/review/08/05/Wheelock.pdf.

Woolley, John T., and Gerhard Peters. The American Presidency Project [online]. University of California, Santa Barbara (hosted), Gerhard Peters (database). www.presidency.ucsb.edu/index.php.

Zinn, Howard, ed. *New Deal Thought.* Indianapolis: Hackett, 2003.

ACKNOWLEDGMENTS

Every book is a team effort. Once again, I was blessed with a dream team at Random House Children's Books. My amazing and ever-dedicated editors: Erin Clarke and Nancy Hinkel. Also precious, the rest of the editorial crew: Rebecca Bullene, Katherine Harrison, and Allison Wortche. And there's the righteous and remarkable designer: Trish Parcell. Krister Engstrom, for his camera skills and help, especially on all those buttons and pinbacks. The inimitable—and relentless—production people: Artie Bennett, Janet Frick, Alison Kolani, Lisa Leventer, Carol Naughton, and Amy Schroeder. And not least, the marvelous postproduction folks: Tracy Lerner, Lisa Nadel, and Adrienne Waintraub.

For going the extra mile when I was researching visuals, thank you so much, Mark Renovitch, at the FDR Presidential Library and Museum. Also: Kristen Lambert at the LBJ Presidential Library and Museum; Barbara Morley at Cornell's Kheel Center; Laura Rosen at the MTA Bridges and Tunnels Special Archive; LaJuan Williams-Dickerson at the FDIC's Public Affairs Office; and at the University of Kentucky Libraries, Jason Flahardy, Jeff Suchanek, and Lewis Warden.

Special thanks to Craig Gropper and Phil Nelson for your generosity; to Brian Carlin, Marsha Green, and Phil Panaritis with the NYC-USDOE's TAH Project for being sounding boards; to John Raby for reading the ARC; and to Jimmy Shepard and Edda Calderon for doing me a super solid when I needed to get up to Hyde Park.

Bobby Thomas: I can't thank you enough for allowing me access, again and again, to your JD and PhD-in-economics brain and then reading the final draft.

ILLUSTRATION CREDITS

*Most images appear with some cropping but without compromising their editorial integrity.
Items not listed are from the author's collection.*

AP Images: 54, 59, 61, 87 (photo of FDR on *Newsweek* cover), and 98; **Archives Center, National Museum of American History, Behring Center, Smithsonian Institution (Scurlock Studio Records):** 99; **Archives of American Art, Smithsonian Institution, courtesy of the William Gropper papers, 1916–1983 (bulk 1926–1977), and used by permission of Craig Gropper** (*New Masses*, March 20, 1934 / Magazine: 31 p.: ill.; 31 x 24 cm): 57; © **Bettmann/Corbis:** 17; **Collection of the Supreme Court of the United States:** 94; **Culver Pictures:** 85 (Coughlin riled up); *The Detroit News:* 19 (silhouetted) and 92; **FDIC:** 49 (seal); **FDR Presidential Library and Museum:** Facing 1, 3, 4 (all), 9 (and used by permission of Hearst Communications, Inc.), 15, 25 (and courtesy of the *Courier-Post*), 28 (and courtesy of Scripps Howard News Service), 30 (fireside chat), 33, 35, 36, 38, 44, 48, 53 (Minneapolis riot), 66, 74, 78 (*Young Tramps*), 79 (*The Emperor's New Clothes* and *Triple-A Plowed Under*), 80 (school lunch and dam), and 81 (NYA library assistants and NYA office workers); **General Douglas MacArthur Foundation:** 10; **Georgia State University Library, Special Collections Department ("Labor, Women Picketers J. Allen Slide," Southern Labor Archives):** 53 (textile workers); **Getty Images:** 5 (Topical Press Agency/Hulton Archive/Getty Images) and 97 (Margaret Bourke-White/Time & Life Pictures/Getty Images); **Kheel Center, Cornell University (Louise Boyle, Photographer, Southern Tenant Farmers' Union Photographs):** 58; **LBJ Library:** 80 (LBJ, photo by unknown); **Library of Congress:** frontispiece, 24, 40, 51, 64, 78 (concert poster), 79 (contest poster), 80 (housing poster and FDR in ND), 84, 88, 90, 91, 102 (poster), and 103 (silhouetted); **MTA Bridges and Tunnels Special Archive (Photographer: O. Winston Link):** 106–107 (gradated); **National Archives and Records Administration:** 80 (Hopkins) and 81 (WPA worker); **Philip I. Nelson, Phil's Old Radios, http://antiqueradio.org:** 30 (radio); **Ohio Historical Society:** 93; **Pars International:** 87 (*Newsweek* logo and layout. From *Newsweek* 11/7/1936 © 1936 Newsweek, Inc. All rights reserved. Used by permission and protected by the Copyright Laws of the United States. The printing, copying, redistribution, or retransmission of the Material without express written permission is prohibited); **San Francisco History Center, San Francisco Public Library:** 53 (Bridges) and 71; **State Archives of Florida:** 22 (silhouetted); **University of Kentucky Libraries, Special Collections and Digital Programs Division:** 57 (pamphlet covers) and 86 (logo); **University of Washington Libraries, Special Collections (Lee 10544A):** 6–7 (gradated); **Vassar College Libraries Archives & Special Collections, Portrait of Hallie Flanagan Davis:** 102; **Wisconsin Historical Society (WHi-37744):** 43; **Wright's Reprints:** 20.

Index